W9-AXA-031

MASTERS AT WORK

3 1526 05542373 2

MASTERS AT WORK

BECOMING A CLIMATE SCIENTIST

KYLE DICKMAN

SIMON & SCHUSTER

New York   London   Toronto   Sydney   New Delhi

Simon & Schuster
1230 Avenue of the Americas
New York, NY 10020

Copyright © 2021 by Simon & Schuster, Inc.

All rights reserved, including the right to reproduce this book
or portions thereof in any form whatsoever. For information, address
Simon & Schuster Subsidiary Rights Department,
1230 Avenue of the Americas, New York, NY 10020.

First Simon & Schuster hardcover edition August 2021

SIMON & SCHUSTER and colophon are registered trademarks of
Simon & Schuster, Inc.

For information about special discounts for bulk purchases,
please contact Simon & Schuster Special Sales at 1-866-506-1949
or business@simonandschuster.com.

The Simon & Schuster Speakers Bureau can bring authors to your
live event. For more information or to book an event, contact the
Simon & Schuster Speakers Bureau at 1-866-248-3049
or visit our website at www.simonspeakers.com.

Manufactured in the United States of America

1   3   5   7   9   10   8   6   4   2

Library of Congress Control number is 1982142642.

ISBN 978-1-9821-4264-3
ISBN 978-1-9821-4265-0 (ebook)

For my parents, Bonnie and Paul,
who taught me the love for the natural world
that I am now passing to my children,
Bridger and Tallie.
This book is also for you two.
May you and your generation have the fortitude,
poise, and will to lead us through
the challenges ahead.

CONTENTS

BECOMING A
CLIMATE SCIENTIST

———————

It's mid-November and snowing lightly in Los Alamos, New Mexico, and the climate scientist Cathy Wilson is inside one of the few low-security buildings at Los Alamos National Laboratory. She's studying a digital model of an Alaskan hillside, the final stage of a project investigating climate change. Four months earlier, Wilson had been on that actual hillside in the Alaskan Arctic, collecting soil samples in a barren valley while a group of musk oxen peered down at her from the ridge above. Today's view is far less exotic. On a laptop screen is an image of a grassy hillside with a strip of shrubs at its base. But this model is exactly the point of that trip.

Wilson is a geomorphologist whose work studying permafrost applies directly to climate science. Although she covers much of the globe for work, she travels most often to the Alaskan Arctic. Wilson's job is to collect accurate data there, but she works closely with modelers, whose job it is to represent her fieldwork as code that can fit into global climate models that forecast the future world. Three modelers, fifteen or more years her junior, are ready to present their models. They seem nervous. Having worked with Wilson for several years now, each knows well that she's uncommonly quick at catching errors and deeply familiar with both the processes they're trying to model and the models themselves. Efficient to the point of bluntness, the modelers agree: Wilson can be intimidating.

"So you mean your active layer depth was too deep on the previous version?" Wilson asks James Joseph Beisman III, an early thirties physicist-turned-modeler with a gray beanie pulled over his straight hair. Beisman, who has a PhD in hydrology, has built a model of one of the five research sites in Alaska where Wilson worked this past summer. Called Teller 27, shorthand for Mile Marker 27 on the Teller Road, the location is near the coast of the Seward Peninsula, a bulb of land about halfway up Alaska that juts into the Bering Sea like the state's nose in profile. The focus of Beisman's model is narrow—to determine how the colonization of shrubs on one slope, in one drainage, of one Arctic peninsula is causing the permafrost to thaw there—but the team's interest in this pan-Arctic process is global. Permafrost, or ground that's been frozen for a very long time, is richer in carbon than any other soil type on the planet; indeed, it contains almost twice the carbon that is already in the atmosphere. When it thaws, the carbon gets released as a greenhouse gas, exacerbating climate change. If Wilson and Beisman can understand how shrubs are contributing to the permafrost's thaw at Teller 27, they can also understand what climate change means for the Arctic's future and what the Arctic's future means for the rest of the world.

Wilson's question to Beisman about the active layer refers to the layer of the permafrost nearest the surface. The active layer thaws each summer and refreezes in the winter. Scientists often use the active layer's depth as a proxy for the frozen ground's health. But Wilson is now asking about how the model was set up. To become a crystal ball, the model must first accurately represent the past and present.

"Oh, yeah, I mean it was, like, 30 meters deep," Beisman says of the active layer depth in previous versions of the model. "But I tweaked the thermal conductance and energy flux to bring it within a meter of the surface." Translation: he adjusted the air temperature and tweaked the rate the ground released the heat, a continual process, until the active layer depth wasn't unrealistically deep and instead looked like what Wilson had observed at Teller 27.

"Aha," she says.

"It paints a really clear picture," Beisman goes on, referring to a key scientific paper that he'd used to build this model. "Where there are shrubs, the ground is warmer, so there's no year-round permafrost there." Then he adds with a wary laugh, "Just in case you didn't know that."

Of course she knew that: Wilson cowrote the paper Beisman had used to build the model. In essence, she'd written the book he's trying to replicate.

CATHY WILSON IS ON the shorter side, with a slight build, a warm smile, and straight silver hair that she keeps stylish and practically cropped just above her ears. She was trained at the University of California, Berkeley, in geomorphology, a science that studies the evolution of land, yet she's the rare field scientist fluent in the language of modelers, a highly technical discipline that requires expertise in computer programming. Today she's wearing black-framed eyeglasses à la Buddy Holly and a gray sweater over business slacks. Like many women who hold high-profile positions in fields dominated by men, Wilson is often the best-dressed person in the room. It is a point of pride for her and befits her position.

At sixty-four, Wilson is a senior research scientist at the Department of Energy's national security–focused Los Alamos National Laboratory (LANL), a position she's held for twenty years. Her job is to study the earth, how it's changing, and what its future may look like. It keeps her on the move. Two days earlier she'd returned from a trip to Washington, D.C., where she met with leaders within the DOE to discuss climate change's impact on energy infrastructure.

The week before that, she'd been in Utqiagvik, Alaska, formerly known as Barrow, where she was giving the DOE's director of the Office of Science a tour of another research site. Earlier this afternoon Wilson had convened seven other senior scientists from various scientific disciplines at LANL to discuss repositioning the lab as the country's leader on climate change solutions. The crux of her argument: with disasters come public questions, and with public questions come scientific opportunities and funding. The age of rapid climate change has only just begun and has already asserted itself as one of the country's most pressing immediate and long-term national security threats. LANL, she argued, should be ready to find answers and become a leader in the field.

But despite the abundance of responsibilities, Wilson's passion is the project she's discussing with the modelers now. Called Next-Generation Ecosystem Experiments Arctic—or NGEE Arctic by the acronym-loving scientists—it is one outsized tentacle in the world's elaborate and rapidly expanding climate research network. For $10 million a year over a decade, the Department of Energy is funding around one hundred scientists from four national labs and the University of Alaska Fairbanks to work on NGEE Arctic. The project's primary mission sits at the heart of all climate science: to collect field observations of essential Arctic processes so that they can make global climate models that better predict the world's future.

Seven years into NGEE Arctic, Beisman's model is a leap toward that eventual conclusion. The equations that power big-picture models utilize hundreds of thousands of data points gathered using drones, satellites, helicopters, and low-elevation flights in bush planes. But they're primarily based on Wilson and her colleagues' fieldwork. Over the past seven years of NGEE Arctic, her team has taken the pulse of Alaska's permafrost by spending weeks each year measuring every possible variable. They dig pits in the frozen ground to describe its essential nature. They sample the air's chemical composition above it or the water percentage of thawed ground at its surface. These tasks and dozens of others are all carried out in conditions that range from record-hot 80°F (26.7°C) Arctic summers to blizzards blowing in temperatures −40°F (−40°C). The work provides a life rich in adventure. While collecting data for NGEE Arctic, Wilson has squared off with musk oxen. She's watched a polar bear feast on a walrus on an ice-strewn beach and Arctic foxes squabbling over the remnants of a caribou. She has climbed into snow caves to get warm on particularly windy afternoons and spent long days dressed from head to toe in mosquito netting to get just a little space from what locals refer to as "Alaska's state bird."

To almost anyone, beholding Beisman's model would be absolutely thrilling. He has breathed digital life into the research Wilson and her team have gathered for almost a decade. But Wilson, now listening intently at the table with her arms crossed and quietly tapping her pen on a notebook, seems mostly concerned. To date, no model exists that captures the dynamics of how shrubs thaw permafrost. And while Beisman's start is promising, the work clearly exemplary, the model still feels too complex, too computationally demanding, to fit into global climate models. The model needs to be simplified.

GLOBAL CLIMATE MODELS ARE the science's most powerful tool. They mimic the earth's complexity, allowing climatologists to select from infinite possibilities the most likely versions of the planet's future. To do this, these programs stitch together leaner versions of higher-fidelity models like the one Wilson and Beisman are now working on with the shrubs. Global climate models represent the earth's surface in 30-by-30 kilometer grid cells. One useful way to think of them is like a composite picture of a certain young man made by assembling together a number of seemingly random yet intentionally selected smaller photographs to result in his image. Each photo can be thought of as both a picture in and of itself and an essential part of the larger image. In global climate models, this example is taken one step further. The code animates these individual pictures through time, with each photo changing subtly, progressively, in relation to the others, until you step back and realize that time has rendered the young man an old man.

While it's hard to imagine how a process as specific to one hillside on one Arctic peninsula could possibly dictate global climate, it does, because global climate is the sum of all its parts. "To get it right, it's all or nothing with global climate models," says Gavin A. Schmidt, a modeler at NASA. "You have to nail all the fine-scale processes to nail the big picture." The relationship between shrubs and permafrost is just one in the tens of millions of fine-scale processes— from methane-digesting microbes in the Congo to whales and dolphins circulating carbon in the ocean—that converge to form our global climate. Globally, tens of thousands of scientists are dedicating their careers to topics like these and countless others related to climate change. Like her colleagues, Wilson is trying to determine if the interaction between permafrost and shrubs absolutely must be included in global climate models.

This holistic view on what shapes climate is relatively new. Broadly defined as average weather over time, the atmosphere used to be the climate scientist's sole playground. But over the past seventy years a scientific revolution has swept the field. Today, climate science is shockingly interdisciplinary.

Interested in studying climate? Pick the science discipline that interests you most—biology, sociology, archaeology, climatology, meteorology, or just about any other ology—and work out from there. You can practice climate science with a bachelor's degree (four years of post–high school education), a master's degree (six to seven years), or a PhD (ten years or more). Cathy Wilson, who has a PhD in geology, finished her education before climate science was even a popular field, a statement that says far more about the recent jumps in the discipline's scientific prominence than Wilson's age.

"I want to make global climate models that help us understand how we're screwing up climate systems," she says. This work is essential. Accurately forecasting climate change could tell us where food production centers may migrate. It will hint at the severity of future floods and droughts, hurricanes, wildfires, and the accelerating pace of the world's ongoing sixth major extinction event. In other words, barring celestial collisions or earthquakes, Wilson wants to play a hand in developing global climate models accurate enough that they can predict when and where Mother Nature's increasingly volatile moods will threaten humanity itself.

Of all places in the world, the Arctic is the earth's canary in the coal mine. That's long been suspected since the climatologist Syukuro Manabe built the first global climate model for the National Weather Service in the 1960s. Since then, computer processing power and knowledge of climate systems has increased exponentially, leading to far more accurate models that have only confirmed his hunch. With the most advanced models now solving as many as 18,000 equations per second for months at a time, climate scientists can peer decades and even centuries into the future of our home planet. (Oddly enough, predictions five years out are harder to make than fifty.) But while the computer and climate science revolutions have filled in the details of global change, the Arctic, so hard to reach and so hard to study, remains climate models' most glaring blind spot.

"We don't have a full understanding of the processes that drive this system. Until we do, we can't accurately represent them in our models," Wilson says. The urgency is real. This summer Arctic lands were about 3.4°F (about 1.9°C) warmer than the average temperatures found between 1981 and 2010, and it's warming two times faster than any other region on earth. From space, the Arctic, growing more hospitable to leafy plants, is visibly greening. With the Bering Sea significantly warmer than just twenty years ago, already 75 percent of the sea ice in the northern hemisphere has melted. Scientists see a similar fate befalling the 22.5 million square kilometers of permafrost.

NGEE Arctic chose permafrost as their focus because of the staggering volume of carbon that frozen ground contains. When permafrost thaws, the carbon it stores gets released as a greenhouse gas, which further accelerates the planet's warming and stokes erratic climate change. Without understanding every link in the chain of reactions that actually cause permafrost to thaw, it's impossible to model with much authority how much greenhouse gas the Arctic will release in the coming decades. Simply put, science cannot fully grasp global climate until it grasps the Arctic. At this moment, current climate models are thought to be underestimating the region's carbon emissions by almost half.

"IT'S A FUNDAMENTAL PROCESS not represented in the models," Wilson says, gesturing toward the shrubs in Beisman's model. He's finished giving Wilson his tour of the model, and she is now making an impassioned case for this narrow model's potentially broad applications, growing animated in the process.

As temperatures have increased in the Arctic over the past four decades, shrubs have expanded northward, invading the once treeless tundra. Satellites have tracked their proliferation, but they didn't see what Wilson has witnessed in the field. Even in places where the permafrost is otherwise intact, the patches of colonizing shrubs have thawed the permafrost underneath, leaving the frozen ground swampy in some places and strangely dry to the touch in others. These holes in the permafrost are spreading with the shrubs. Warmer temperatures are ushering in more shrubs and more alders in particular, which are injecting nitrogen into the Arctic's nitrogen-starved soils, which invites more plants to grow, which speeds the permafrost's thaw, which releases more carbon into the atmosphere, which causes the temperatures to warm more and faster, which invites more shrubby alders to grow. Wilson is relaying a version of this process to the modelers in staccato, with the main point being this: more shrubs means less permafrost and more atmospheric carbon dioxide. Then she pauses and shrugs.

"Unless, of course, it doesn't work like that at all," she says. Instead, she asks, what if the colonizing alder shrubs actually photosynthesize the extra carbon that the thawing permafrost is emitting, turning the Arctic into a forest that balances the earth's carbon budget, working to slow climate change? Climate is complicated. "That's exactly why we're studying it," Wilson notes.

It's a tidy summation of climate science. The world's far too complicated to grasp at a glance. To understand how it all fits together, every piece must be isolated, scrutinized, represented by code, and nested into its rightful place in a model that does its best to mimic the actual world. Some of these pieces won't ever make it into global climate models, but there's simply no way to know how the world fits together until it's studied.

Wilson has earned this deep understanding through years of building and tweaking models. But, more than anything, it has required an even more intimate connection to the frozen ground itself.

t's a bright and windless morning in August, four months before the modeling meeting, and Wilson is kneeling beside Emma Lathrop, Wilson's twenty-two-year-old research assistant and her constant companion in the field. Lathrop is about to sink a three-foot-long thermometer into Alaska's recently thawed permafrost for the forty-third time today. It's data collection season. The women are working at the foot of a hill called Kougarok. The hill rises from tussock tundra about eighty miles northwest of Nome, a gold-mining town connected to the outside world only by an airport and a harbor often made impassable by sea ice. This is the sixth trip Wilson has made to Kougarok in six years. As with her other trips, the landscape looks markedly different since her last visit. After a record snowpack and an unseasonably strong rain two weeks earlier, the polar desert is shimmering with even more water than usual. Lathrop buries the thermometer in the ground and the recently thawed permafrost gushes like a wet sponge.

Bob Bolton and Xiaoying Jin, two scientists from the

University of Alaska Fairbanks, have joined Wilson and Lathrop in the field today to collect data for the NGEE Arctic project. The land is empty, wild, and breathtaking. There's a moose browsing the willows beside a clear river and the scientists are the only humans in a view without end. Wilson and NGEE Arctic's other project leaders chose Kougarok—one of five research sites in Alaska that will collectively reshape how climate models represent the Arctic—in large part because it sits near permafrost's southern boundary around latitude 66°30' N, the line that officially marks the Arctic Circle.

At certain times of the year, the hill is rigged with so much equipment that it resembles a patient in an intensive care unit. There are cameras to document the seasonal changes of plants; watch-size sensors that measure the photosynthesis of leaves, take the temperature, or monitor the soil moisture at the roots of shrubs. On top of the hill is a remote weather station recording everything from solar radiation to ground and air temperatures. Meanwhile, at that moment, satellites festooned with instrumentation are passing over the North Pole, their sensors trained on Kougarok to see if it's possible to collect the frozen ground's vital signs from space.

What makes this hill so fascinating to these scientists is that it's indistinguishable from the landscape around it. In the language of climate science, it is "representative" of this portion of the Seward Peninsula and, therefore, of a certain swath of the Arctic. Kougarok is a bump in a wide valley that's rimmed to the west by 3,000-foot sawtooth mountains and to the east by long, undulating hills left there by retreating glaciers at the end of the last ice age. Tufts of ankle-high grasses, called tussocks, for which the tussock tundra is named, cover almost everything. In the cooler and shadier places of the hill, young alder shrubs grow. A stand of alders grows atop Kougarok, blocking the view to the west of frigid meltwater ponds and the thousands of sandhill cranes wading in them. The birds' garbled chatter rides on a breeze blowing in from the Bering Sea. Most of the morning, this brisk wind kept the insects at bay, but soon the winds begin to die down and a swarm of tiny bugs emerge from some hidden hollow in the tundra. Soon enough, one finds the corner pocket of Wilson's left eye and she tries to blink it out.

"Zero," says Lathrop, reading the temperature in Celsius off the thermometer.

"Zero," Wilson repeats, sweeping the bug out with her pinky finger, then jotting the number in her notebook. This morning she's wearing a floppy safari-style hat and a blue Patagonia puffy jacket. Zero degrees Celsius indicates Lathrop hit the active layer, that top strata of frozen ground that thaws in summer and refreezes when the cold returns. For a sense of what the permafrost looks like and the active layer's relation to it, imagine taking a cross section of the ground. Farther to the south, the shallower permafrost is called "discontinuous" and looks like a Dalmatian: mostly frozen ground separated by spots of cold dirt and rocks. In a gradient moving northward, the permafrost becomes more continuous, sinking as deep as a half mile below the surface in the far north. The active layer floats across all this in the summer, a veneer of ground that freezes and thaws with annual temperature changes. It would be impossible to get a reliable measurement of how deep the permafrost goes. But by measuring the active layer depth here at Kougarok, Wilson can get a read on the permafrost's health: Did more of it thaw this year than historically? This summer the answer is unequivocally yes.

"Certainly not what we saw last year," says Wilson, opting to avoid jumping to conclusions, as any good scientist does. But it suggests that this summer's heavy rains and historically warm temperatures drove the active layer deeper, shrinking the permafrost further. Wilson can see this, too, but she can't interpret a data point until she's fixed it to a trend line based on other data.

By the time NGEE Arctic is complete, Wilson and her team will have collected measurements relevant to the health of Kougarok's permafrost twice a year—one of snow depth at the end of winter and one of active layer depth in late summer—for three years. These measurements and others will be used to assemble a coherent story, one that will explain the order and magnitude of the processes driving the seismic change sweeping southern Alaska's permafrost. If trying to write an entire landscape's story with data collected on six days spread across three years sounds like reconstructing Beethoven's forty-minute Seventh Symphony from a few wayward notes heard from the *Moonlight Sonata*, you've got it about right. That's science, though. For many reasons— location, weather, manpower, logistics, cost—it's impossible to continuously monitor all of the earth all of time, so earth system scientists do the best they can. They take strategic snapshots of the landscape at critical moments and extrapolate the larger story, constantly amending their conclusions as more information comes in. "Science is self-correcting," a phrase Wilson and others in her field use like a mantra.

NGEE Arctic has six central research questions exploring precisely how climate change will impact the Arctic, and Wilson's research will answer one of them. Hers is a play on those five *W*'s every newspaper story includes in the first paragraph: Where, when, and why will the Arctic get wetter or drier? To answer these questions, the measurements she's taken include, among other things, the thickness of the active layer, the location of shrubs, snow depth, and the soil moisture found in places representative of the greater

Arctic. This data, she hopes, will point to what could happen when the permafrost, which gives the land its structure, thaws. Will the land collapse and deform? Where will the water go? Will it pool atop the remaining ice as if it were in a bathtub, leaving the soil wet? Or will it escape, draining into aquifers or other micro-watersheds, leaving the soil dry? If dry, thawed permafrost tends to emit more carbon dioxide. If wet, it also emits methane, a chemical closely related to carbon dioxide that is four times more potent as a greenhouse gas. "You start to see why all this stuff that seems so insignificant matters," she says. "Water is the key to everything."

To collect the wide array of data from Kougarok needed to answer these questions, Wilson set up ten 60-meter-long transects, or sample areas, that were representative of the hill's various slopes, elevations, aspects, and soil and vegetation types. Every fifteen meters along those transects, they sampled the earth, creating a pattern of perforations that would capture any variation in the soil moisture. Historically, Wilson estimates the ground at Kougarok was frozen 40 meters down, with its active layer depth, the thawed ground in summer, normally around 30 centimeters below the surface. This summer the average at Kougarok was 70 centimeters—twice as deep as when they measured it in 2017. Put simply, the permafrost in this spot was thawing incredibly quickly, maybe even disappearing. It's a localized symptom of climate change emblematic of what's happening across the Arctic.

This year, 2019, was the warmest year for the northern hemisphere in 140 years of record keeping. The same week that Wilson took the temperature of the slushy ground outside Nome, historically large fires in the boreal forest outside of Anchorage forced thousands of Alaskans to evacuate. Across the Bering Strait, almost 2 million acres of Siberia's permafrost burned that summer, much of it for the first time on record. A few months later, 30 million acres caught fire in Australia. These fires compounded the amount of greenhouse gases adrift in the atmosphere; not only were the fires belching all the carbon that the trees had stored over their sixty- to hundred-year life spans, but they were also erasing the forest's ability to store carbon in the future.

A similar phenomenon could be observed with the thawing permafrost. Permanently frozen soils contain between 20,000 and 50,000 years of carbon, the remnants of long dead plants and animals. When these soils thaw, not only do they stop storing carbon recently emitted by humans, but what used to be a carbon sink turns into an emissions faucet. "How big is that faucet? How much carbon dioxide and how much methane is it going to be pouring into the atmosphere?" Wilson asks. "If we continue emitting greenhouse gases at the rate we're emitting today, we're going to lose most of the permafrost in the Arctic."

———

WILSON DOESN'T IMMEDIATELY COME across as the intellectual powerhouse that she is. Her manner is generally curious and conversational, and in certain situations she can be warm and even motherly. ("I can't help myself," she says, growing animated in mock defense after once fixing me a sandwich for a field lunch. "I'm a boomer mom.") But like many high-achieving women, she can turn matter-of-fact quickly. During the biannual data-collecting trips necessary for her job, Wilson works sixteen-hour days and routinely loses five pounds because she forgets to eat. For better or worse, when working, accomplishing her task becomes paramount to everything else.

She would describe herself as rigorous. Her colleagues use different descriptors: type A; brilliant; a detail-oriented perfectionist who, like many good scientists, sometimes tilts toward obsessive-compulsiveness; a rule follower; a stickler for safety; a striver. Her nickname among NGEE Arctic team members is "Full Throttle." The title captures well the competition and drive she brings to her work. The fact of her success often flies in the face of the warm, nurturing, and friendly behavior expected of American women, a stereotype upheld in the scientific community. Unlike Wilson's male peers, those she works with rarely describe her as likable. Instead, some find her forceful leadership style off-putting. What they don't say, but is probably closer to the truth, is that, in the male-dominated world of science, Wilson's aptitude and success is threatening. "She's had to fight long and hard to get where she is," says Bob Bolton. That route has forged her leadership style.

Like most climate scientists, Wilson wasn't trained to be a climate scientist. "It's just what I tell people I am when I'm riding the chairlift," she says. "You can be a climate scientist today in any earth science discipline as long as you're applying your disciplinary expertise to bigger picture questions." Wilson's disciplinary expertise is geomorphology, or the study of landscape evolution, with a particular emphasis on the role of water. She never expected to become one of the world's top permafrost experts. Wilson grew up a math nerd in California who studied theater arts in college; built cars in Grand Blanc, Michigan, as the first female shift boss in a General Motors factory; and worked for the oil company Chevron before becoming a climate scientist at one of the world's most distinguished research institutions. It wasn't until she began studying for a PhD that she started to realize that some of the traits that irked her about herself also made her particularly well suited to her chosen profession.

For example, Wilson has an eye for detail and an aversion to diverging from plans, a combination maddening when following a recipe in the kitchen but useful when practicing science in the field. She also has an aptitude for scaling between ideas big and small; an unquenchable thirst for understanding how systems both man-made and natural work; a hard-headed stubbornness that served her well during the eleven years of post–high school education required to earn a PhD; and a fearless confidence in her own ability to grasp complex ideas, even those outside her area of study. The winding path Wilson has taken to her career's apex has forced upon her an appreciation that no career trajectory is strictly upward. Achieving success, she knows, requires grit and the ability to get comfortable with being uncomfortable.

Although constantly being physically and mentally tested throughout her career, she perhaps felt it most while working toward her PhD at Berkeley. Her dissertation studied the contributing triggers to landslides. Not only did this require that she assemble relevant pieces from many different data streams into a single cohesive story, a skill set essential for her current work, it also meant that she had to spend days in the rain collecting thousands of water pressure measurements that could then be projected onto an entire drainage system. After a week of working night and day in a ceaseless winter rain, she contracted pneumonia. "I loved it!" Wilson says in hindsight. "It was so fascinating figuring out how small pieces fit into the larger scheme. Also adventurous. Also fun. Also hard. Also scary to be alone in the rain on a dark mountainside with just a lantern to light my way."

"That's what makes Cathy," said Bob Bolton as they worked in the field around Nome. "Whatever she does, she's going to do it to the absolute best of her ability."

While Wilson eats lunch on the ridgetop with a view of the Arctic spilling out in all directions, Bolton—who, in his late forties, is tall and lean—decides to hike out to the micro-meteorological station on Kougarok's summit to check the instruments, which measure relative humidity, precipitation, ground and air temperature, solar radiation components, and snow depth. Tufts of musk ox fur were embedded in the rain catchment basin. "They're always using it as a scratching post," he says, pulling the fur out and letting the wind strip it from his fingers like a feather. Bolton says that Wilson is the only senior scientist he works with who can describe in detail how the technical instruments that they use in the field actually work, which would be akin to a programmer being able to explain the exact processes that allow RAM to power their computers. It's a remarkably useful skill set, he points out, because it allows her to diagnose problems in the data and then straighten them into storylines that can be represented in models. But it's also helpful for teasing apart trends that may otherwise be obscured. She sees both the forest and the trees, he explains: she can place fine scale details into the bigger picture without losing sight of the importance of either. "Honestly, it's sort of amazing," he says. "In terms of reputation, knowledge, her ability to do the technical work, there just aren't too many scientists out there like her."

"PUT ON YOUR GLOVES, Emma, please," Wilson reminds Lathrop. After lunch, Wilson and Lathrop begin work on another transect at Kougarok, this one off the east side of the hill's rocky peak. Lathrop is holding a heavy steel rod and preparing to sink it into the ground. Because the thermometers are made of fiberglass and easily broken, step one of taking the ground's temperature is first perforating the ground with the rod to make a hole for the thermometer to go into. Lathrop has spent weeks performing this procedure and responds to Wilson's directive with a dismissive "Mmm" but says nothing and puts the gloves on anyway. After so many unbroken hours working together, the relationship between the two is loving and testy, not unlike a mother and daughter's.

If Wilson has successfully climbed to near the top of her almost forty-year career, Lathrop is on the first pitch and ascending quickly. At just twenty-two, she is a head taller than Wilson, with curly hair, a quick wit, and an inquisitive mind. Lathrop is a post-baccalaureate researcher, an entry-level position that almost every scientist—regardless of the field—occupies some version of early in their career. Self-deprecatingly, she calls her job "scientific grunt labor." She's not wrong, but while balancing on a pair of tussocks she observes that "everybody in science does grunt work." Sometimes the experience is incredible, such as when they fly helicopters into research sites. Sometimes it's unforgettable, as it was two days earlier when her bear spray went off in her backpack, leaving her eyes burning and clothes saturated with the liquid. And sometimes it's miserable, like it was the week before, when it rained nonstop, or the winter before, when the temperature dropped to 4°F and the water in her backpack froze.

The spot Wilson and Lathrop are probing now is a shallow depression about forty meters down the transect. A blueberry bush is growing in the depression and Lathrop, in rubber boots, is standing on top of the bush, sinking a steel rod through its branches. The rod sinks several centimeters down, then stops abruptly. Lathrop grunts, pulls the rod up, and probes again in a slightly different place. Again it stops. "Rocks," she says, having long since learned to distinguish between the way the steel rings and vibrates against rocks and how it thuds and sticks when hitting ice. Having spent three decades experiencing the drudgery that forms the backbone of field science, Wilson is generally happy to let her younger associate do the physical labor. She's now squatting beside Lathrop, plucking small and seedy wild blueberries off a bush.

"Sometimes I collect them for my breakfast cereal," she explains, considering one closely before eating it. Lathrop sinks the rod again, about two inches away from the first two holes, and finally hits ice. She exhales heavily, sweeps the hair out of her face, and pulls the rod out of the hole. Like a metal spoon fresh out of the freezer, it's cold to the touch. The two women then fall into a well-choreographed routine that helps ensure all the relevant data gets logged. Lathrop tosses the steel rod onto another blueberry bush and sinks the more fragile thermometer into the hole in the active layer she just made.

"Thirty-two centimeters," she says, her head inches above the ground as she reads off the ruler etched into the probe's shaft.

"Thirty-two centimeters," Wilson repeats in confirmation, then jots a number onto a Rite in the Rain data sheet with a Rite in the Rain pen. "They're all I use out here," she says, wagging the pen back and forth. Over the years, these two have developed comically strong preferences for all the equipment they carry into the field, from jackets and boots to maps with or without a plastic covering. Wilson has a laminated map of the Kougarok site in her backpack that she likes because the plastic protects the paper from the rain; Lathrop can't stand the plastic—and has forcefully and amusingly told Wilson as much—because the sun glares off it in the summer, making it too hard to read.

"Zero," Lathrop calls out when the thermometer finishes taking the ground temperature.

"Zero degrees," Wilson repeats. She adds the number to a growing spreadsheet unintelligible to all but a small handful of people in the entire world. Some scientists call such hyper-specific numbers "nerd hieroglyphics." For Wilson and Lathrop, this invaluable data is the gold they've come to the Seward Peninsula to mine. Having collected all they need from these three pencil-size holes in the tundra, each woman slings a backpack full of extra layers of clothing, snacks, spare pencils, bear spray, matches, a knife, and a first aid kit over her shoulder, hefts their scientific instruments, plucks one last blueberry for the hike, and moves five meters down the transect to do it all again.

One would think covering such short ground would be anticlimactic. It isn't, because walking in tussock tundra is like crossing a field of cabbages by only stepping on the vegetable heads. Everyone stumbles. "Punching Tussocks," Lathrop calls out as she goes down.

"It'd be a good name for a band!" Wilson suggests. Having once been a singer in a group of musically inclined geologists who called themselves the GeoTones, she considers herself the team's resident expert on punny band names.

There is no archetype of a good climate scientist, but these women, with their sense of humor, certainly embody some of the traits that help. Many climate scientists are outdoorsy, adventurous, and highly organized. They tend to have a keen eye for detail and are intensely curious, using science as their license to contribute novel insights into how the world works. Wilson is a 5.10b traditional rock climber; Lathrop's a skier and hiker. Even in her early sixties, Wilson remains an early adopter of new technologies and loves rap music. (When she gets angry, she raps and dances to a DeJ Loaf song called "Back Up" that sounds like rage rap. Ironically, she never learned to type and still has to hunt and peck.) On the long drives to work sites, they've been listening to Malcolm Gladwell podcasts and a revisionist history of the Boston Tea Party, both of which give them fodder for the ongoing conversations that fill their days in the field. They also tell lots of stories. At one point Wilson shares one about a recent kayaking trip off Washington State's Orcas Island when a pod of killer whales surfaced around her and her husband. Lathrop shares how her work makes her boyfriend, a ski patroller, jealous. ("Hot loads in particular," she says, referring to the winter sampling campaign when the Seward Peninsula's roads are snowed in and they are flown in to the field sites in a helicopter. "We get to board when the rotors are still spinning and he doesn't get to do that as a ski patroller.") To pass the time, they sing. The mood is light and fun; the good weather helps.

"You get kind of delirious in the field," Lathrop laughs, clearly enjoying a sense of dissociation.

"Honestly, I find the repetitiveness kind of meditative," Wilson says of data collection: Frost probe in, frost probe out, data collected, move on. "It gets you out of your head. You're just out here seeing what happens."

MOST DAYS AREN'T SO meditative. The more senior Wilson has grown in her career, the less actual data collection and processing samples she does and the more managing of junior staff and projects. Wilson works in Los Alamos National Laboratory's Earth and Environmental Sciences division, or EES. Her building is one trailer—in what the scientists there affectionately call "the trailer park"—that sits on a mesa in Los Alamos with a view of the Rockies to the east. It houses about sixty scientists and staff, most working on projects related to climate. Among them are a decade-long study of the world's other great carbon sink, the tropical rain forests; a program that manages the mind-numbingly complex logistics of shipping scientific equipment (some hazardous, much of it causing bureaucratic headaches) to some of the world's most remote locations; and a project using directed evolution to generate a soil microbiome that will support crop survival in a drier world. For one year Wilson was the acting deputy division leader of EES, but after the lab hired another person for the role, she "went back to the bench," she says. "I was incredibly disappointed I didn't get the job." But as with other setbacks she's faced, she found new opportunities afterward. She is now the president of the United States Permafrost Association and was appointed by the National Academy of Sciences to an eight-year term on the International Arctic Science Committee, which coordinates international Arctic research efforts.

As with most careers in earth system sciences, Wilson is responsible for finding funding for her projects. She does this by winning grants from various government agencies and by helping industries understand how climate change may impact their business. "So much of climate science is soft money," Bolton says, meaning grant money that scientists have to apply for. "The job demands that you get comfortable with instability—moving from funding source to funding source. It's always stressful trying to constantly sell your ideas. I've contended that being a university soft-money researcher can't be full-time because there's a hole in funding, or you're just going to have a noncreative time, or something else becomes hot and your money shifts away."

Wilson has never had much trouble finding money. Before NGEE Arctic, she worked on several projects investigating how climate change will affect power and energy generation for Wyoming and the Four Corners region of the Southwest—projects that advance the Department of Energy's mission. Recently, Wilson won a substantial grant to conduct research on the impact of climate change on national security issues, a job that takes her to Washington, D.C., often.

These grants pay for not only her salary but the salaries of staff like Lathrop. Other staff include technicians with bachelor's or master's degrees who specialize in data collection, drone operators for remote sensing, statistical experts, and postdoctoral researchers responsible for designing experiments that are often housed within Wilson's larger projects. Wilson helps plot career courses for all of the people who work for her. She helps them set goals and steers their energies down pathways that are most likely to produce scientific publications, the field's highest currency. Her job's day-to-day varies widely. One day she may never leave her office. This can mean hours of conference calls, meeting with technicians to tease out the trends in data, or dealing with finances in her office. But the work often requires travel. Including the field campaigns to Alaska, Wilson spends upward of four months on the road each year. "I'm often most productive on flights, because it's one of the few times I won't be interrupted at work," she says.

Like many Americans, Wilson's job became her identity: not only a critical source of her family's income but her life's purpose. Since grad school Wilson estimates that she's worked between sixty and seventy hours a week, which is about on par with most people in a research profession. "I have a hard time saying no to projects that interest me," she admits. She sees the travel and the work as a perk of the job: a chance to learn new things and interact with new people and ideas. She insists that she isn't a workaholic, although, she acknowledges, "My husband might hold a different opinion." By the end of a long day sticking a giant thermometer into a soggy tussock in the Alaskan tundra, she'll be exhausted. On the drive back to Nome, she'll graze on peanut butter pretzels and Cheetos while contently listening to a podcast on nuclear warfare. After thirty years, field research remains the job's great joy.

"You've got to see the earth in all its glory before it's all gone!" she says now, nearing the final few points in a transect. Wilson extends her arms and spins with a cinematic flourish appropriate to such a dramatic landscape. As she turns toward the rolling hills in the east, a northern harrier lifts off the tussocks, its wingbeats long, lumbering, a bit clumsy. Barely twenty feet off the ground, the raptor stiffens its wings and begins to glide, pivoting its tail back and forth as it rudders effortlessly on the thermals rising off the thawing permafrost.

3

The seed for NGEE Arctic was planted back in the winter of 2008. That's when around fifty earth-system scientists and modelers from the DOE's national labs met at a hotel in Arlington, Virginia, a short drive from the Department of Energy's headquarters. The Climate and Environmental Sciences Division at the DOE funds their most-coveted projects in ten-year blocks. In 2008, the scientists' task was to discuss where to focus their attention between 2010 and 2020. Climate change immediately rose to the top of the pile, but it took three days of discussions to land on the Arctic as one of the places most deserving of the DOE's scientific heft. It was one of the world's greatest carbon sinks and among the least understood places on the planet; NGEE Arctic was funded to clarify scientific mysteries about the region. The trouble was, while many of the scientists were leading experts in their various disciplines—hydrology, plant physiology, geochemistry—the Arctic was an environment with no earthly parallel. When it came to studying frozen ground, the scientists were newbies.

Wilson didn't even attend the meeting. She was concentrating on the desert. "I would have described myself mainly as a temperate hydrologist," she says. "But I'm very much an opportunist. I love doing different things." By 2008, after eight years of working at Los Alamos National Laboratory, Wilson had established herself as a builder of large-scale scientific projects. Rather than a scientist strictly focused on writing papers for esteemed research journals, a common path in climate sciences, she was a proven program developer who turned research ideas into funded projects. She made things happen. At the time, Wilson was focused on projects far closer to home and in a stage of her career that in hindsight she refers to as her transition from hydrologist to climate scientist. One project, called the Energy-Water Nexus, looked at how future droughts would affect power generation and water supply for the people of the Southwest. Before that, she'd studied post-wildfire processes in canyons in Los Alamos, how logging impacted erosion in Tasmania, and how landslides were triggered in California. When she first heard stirrings of NGEE Arctic, she wasn't put off by her lack of experience in the area and saw only an opportunity that LANL didn't want to miss. The DOE had already tipped their hand that they wanted to invest $10 million a year for ten years in the project. That type of money brought stability to enterprising scientists. That type of money enabled scientists to pursue research that made their careers.

At Los Alamos, some of Wilson's colleagues were already studying the Arctic, Antarctica, sea ice, and glaciers—"all the frozen stuff on earth except permafrost," Wilson says. The understudied landform was growing in importance for the climate sciences, so she launched into what would be a four-year process of positioning LANL and herself as permafrost experts. The trick for her would be applying what she already understood deeply—hydrology and geomorphology—to the north. She started by reading all the published scientific literature on Arctic processes she could find.

By the late 2000s the Arctic was flashing dire symptoms of global warming. With the region already warming at twice the rate of the rest of the globe, climate change had begun reorganizing entire ecosystems. The sea ice that once froze over the Bering Sea each winter was fast disappearing, 75 percent of its historic coverage gone by 2019. The fish populations that the region's subsistence-people depend on—as do the fishing industries that feed the rest of the country—were shifted north by warming seas, disrupting traditional ways of life and Alaska's $5.4 billion commercial industry, the source of 60 percent of America's seafood.

Weather patterns seemed to be shifting, too, replacing weeks of subzero winter temperatures with regular storms that were warm and wet. For the plants and animals adapted to the extreme and narrow conditions of the Arctic, warming temperatures were coming at a whiplash pace and pushing Arctic-adapted species to the brink of extinction. No part of the frozen north was unchanged. The population of Canada's ivory gulls fell 70 percent over the past forty years. Across the permafrost, the shift in temperatures reordered the Arctic, benefiting shrubs while shrinking the tundra grasses that formed the biological bases of many northern ecosystems. By 2019, thawing permafrost would be leaching somewhere between 300 and 600 million tons of carbon into the atmosphere each year.

For the eight countries with legal claims to Arctic lands, a geopolitical horse race developed over the wealth of mineral resources and new shipping lanes that climate change was in the process of transforming. And over the past twenty years, as climate change has shifted from abstraction to reality, these countries invested significant resources in researching the Arctic. Russia was already invested: there, thawed permafrost in Siberia is collapsing into sinkholes—and with it, at the cost of billions of dollars, the infrastructure built on top. Greenland, whose melting ice sheets were just beginning to contribute to sea-level rise, had become a magnet for international climate change researchers. Germany's Alfred Wegener Institute would soon be planning an expedition to embed an icebreaking ship in the sea ice for the entire polar winter of

2019 and 2020. From the United States, NASA had already begun rolling out a series of decadal remote sensing studies that leaned on satellites and a fleet of aircraft. Scientific uncertainty and global competition meant deep pockets were opening for research, especially those resources of the national security–focused LANL and the energy-concerned DOE.

"Suddenly there was funding available for projects that we couldn't dream of a decade earlier," says Larry Hinzman, an Arctic researcher from the University of Alaska Fairbanks who has studied the region for thirty years. He's tall and bald, in his mid-sixties, with a quiet voice and disarming manner. In 2009, Hinzman began cooking up a plan to teach global climate modelers how to better represent his backyard. He held a conference with climate modelers in Montreal to ask them what they felt was missing from current models. Wilson attended as part of her Arctic-focused reeducation and, while there, saw some of these shortcomings firsthand. Even in the best models, the Arctic was being represented by taking pieces from different ecosystems, like the American plains, and imprinting them over the colder climates of the north. When snow fell in models, rather than accounting for how topography, aspect, vegetation, and winds distribute snow in the real world, it fell across the landscape in an even sheet. Vegetation in the models was depicted only as bare grass, shrubs, or "Arctic grass" and didn't include any of the actual processes in which various plants take up carbon, fix nitrogen, or trap snow at different rates. Largely missing from the models: the contributions that carbon-rich soils make to atmospheric greenhouse gases; how heat is transferred from air to soil; and, crucially, how water moves through the landscape—all essential when determining climate. "We need to fix this!" Hinzman argued during a talk at the conference. "Until we do, we really can't know what's going to happen to the Arctic."

At that point, "Cathy stood up and said that we didn't have the scientific understanding to create that kind of model," Hinzman remembers with a laugh. "Science just didn't yet grasp how Arctic plants evolved, how photosynthesis worked, how it changed based on vegetation, how the carbon burns off, and how all of it affects the way the climate is going to change. It was so much more complex than any of us expected."

After the conference, Hinzman put together a proposal to the National Science Foundation for a campaign that would collect data in the Arctic on these understudied processes to construct a new, more accurate model of Arctic land. At its core was an idea new to climate science. They'd first study the models and use the gaps in the models' representation of the Arctic to pick where to focus their observational research. "The models drove the observations," says Hinzman.

"They showed us what was missing." Like about half of all of the proposals scientists write, it was rejected. NSF preferred to invest elsewhere. Although he didn't know it at the time, Hinzman had drafted a proposal that would become the basis of NGEE Arctic's research, the most ambitious terrestrial climate science ever conducted in the Arctic.

Wilson's first big opportunity in the Arctic came in 2009. That year Senator Pete Domenici (R-NM), a key member of the Senate Committee on Energy and Natural Resources, pulled down a onetime $5 million earmark for LANL to study climate science. Wilson, who had worked closely with the senator on the Energy-Water Nexus project, was put in charge of the money. She invested part of it in a place that at first seemed odd. For many years a colleague in LANL's Earth and Environmental Sciences division named Bryan Travis had been developing a model of Mars's permafrost. Wilson recognized that because, as one modeler put it, "we haven't found yet a planet where the laws of physics don't apply," it should work for the Earth's permafrost too. "Part of what I've loved to do throughout my career is go between the management and the bench, or the scientists in our division, and build projects that can bring in money," Wilson says. She recognized this as one of those opportunities.

Wilson used Travis's model as a stepping stone for positioning LANL as the DOE's top permafrost lab. From that initial earmark, she invested around $1 million dollars and three years into getting Travis's model to answer fairly basic questions about the earth's permafrost. This work planted the seed for a more ambitious project that would result in a novel new code called the Arctic Terrestrial Simulator, a permafrost-focused model without parallel. It included many of the coupled processes that Hinzman recognized as missing but critical and served as a template for studying other ecosystems. (The project won a coveted R&D 100 Award in 2020.) Today, that fine-scale model resolves processes like hydrology, thermal and heat transfer, snow redistribution, vegetation dynamics, and carbon cycling that occur at scales from a meter to hundreds of meters. Most important, it does all this in three dimensions so that it can predict how the permafrost will become deformed when it thaws. That information is incredibly useful for understanding how processes work and their relationship to each other. "Nobody else could model permafrost in the detail that we were modeling it," Wilson says.

By the fall of 2009, the DOE had put Stan D. Wullschleger, a forest biologist at Oak Ridge National Laboratory near Knoxville, Tennessee, in charge of NGEE Arctic. Wullschleger, a brilliant scientist by reputation, was also a gifted project leader. He had just finished running a historic DOE experiment, for which he and a team had designed large open-top chambers to study warming forested ecosystems. The design was intended to be used in a future experiment to warm spruce trees in Minnesota.

"They wanted to repeat the experiment in the Arctic. They'd planned these huge 10-meter-diameter chambers that they'd put on top of the permafrost," Hinzman says. "It really wasn't a good design for the Arctic at all." Wilson used the predecessor of the Arctic Terrestrial Simulator, the Mars permafrost model, to see what would happen if they built carbon dioxide and heating chambers atop the permafrost. It was just as Hinzman predicted. "They generated so much heat, they burned a hole straight through the frozen ground," Wilson says with a laugh. "The whole experiment was literally going to collapse!"

After the model's findings, the chamber plan was understandably scrapped. Around that time, Wullschleger came out to LANL for a three-day visit with Wilson. He says that was when she distinguished herself as a very able and willing participant in the project—a team leader. "Her breadth of understanding was more appealing than any single depth she had. More general to earth system processes, she simply appreciated how multiple areas of science needed to come together to answer some of these complex, system-level challenges," Wullschleger explains. Soon after, he asked Wilson if she'd be willing to be LANL's lead scientist on the project.

She would be in charge of a budget of $2.2 million a year if they won the proposal.

With so many pieces of a sprawling project beginning to fit together, the DOE committed a year's worth of pre-funding to research the proposal. Now they just had to finish writing it.

FROM THE WINDOW SEAT of the prop plane, Alaska looked every bit as stunning as Wilson had hoped. It was mid-August 2011, about six months after Stan Wullschleger had asked her to join the NGEE Arctic project. This was her first field trip to the Arctic. The plane was skimming north over the Brooks Range's 9,000-foot peaks, which run from east to west across the top third of Alaska. The Arctic Ocean shimmered on the horizon, and Wilson's eyes picked out the black squares of grazing musk oxen and a herd of caribou migrating north toward greener grasslands. Below the plane, a patchwork of Arctic diversity scrolled by. Climate science is about uncovering patterns in nature, and with each new vista came new questions: Why do we see shrubs on the hill slopes and in the bottoms of drainages but nowhere else? How much water is out there and does the volume change during the year? Why are there so many different colors on the landscape? And how does all this flow together to influence climate?

The experience was much the same for each of the nine senior scientists whom Wullschleger had asked to join the flight. The sheer number of questions was intimidating. *How are we going to go about representing the entire Arctic in models?* Wullschleger remembers thinking during the flight. "It was a real mix of exciting and daunting, though I admit I felt mostly the latter." Since Wullschleger had last seen Wilson, he'd flown to six national labs and expanded the project's scope to include hydrologists, geologists, geomorphologists, biogeochemists, and vegetation dynamics experts. He also invited the University of Alaska Fairbanks's International Arctic Research Center and Hinzman, who'd recently been promoted to director of the center, to serve as the DOE's partners and Arctic experts.

That key idea that Hinzman had struck on in Montreal three years earlier—that a lack of fundamental understanding of Arctic processes was at the core of poor modeling and that the existing models could help show them where the largest knowledge gaps lay—had been adopted as the centerpiece of NGEE Arctic's mission. The task now was figuring out which processes held the most sway over climate, measuring them in discrete ecosystem types, and then scaling those processes up. The NGEE team knew they couldn't measure every inch of the Arctic. Accomplishing their mission required the team to be deliberate about where they conducted their research.

In the weeks before the flight, Wilson had been studying the work of an Arctic scientist named Torre Jorgensen. For the past thirty years Jorgensen had been flying bush planes or helicopters to places that struck him as interesting and then jumping out and collecting samples by the thousands. In doing so, he'd developed a concept of ecosystem types where climate, geology, biochemistry, hydrology, soils, plants, and geochemistry all coevolved in a particular place. In other words, everything in an ecosystem is dependent on other organisms in the ecosystem; when one thing changes, everything else changes with it. If the scientists could figure out how all the pieces fit together in a specific Arctic ecosystem type, they could build a model that showed how webs of systems connect, and by doing so model the entire Arctic. "This sat smack dab in the middle of how geomorphologists think about the problem," Wilson says. "There's structure to the way the landscape organizes itself." Like a hunter field dressing an animal, they couldn't cut up every small piece of meat and carry it out individually. Instead, they had to divide the landscape up into large, related classes—legs (high-elevation tundra), neck (coastal hills), back (permafrost)—and then study only the pieces they expected to influence global climate the most.

To begin the process of selecting which places to study, the NGEE team used an algorithm-driven technique called multivariate spatio-temporal clustering. Using thirty-seven different variables that ranged from geology to plant communities, the algorithm took layers and layers of Alaska's existing scientific maps and divided the state into broadly related ecoregions: places that shared many of the same features. The program divided Alaska into twenty landscape types and found five different classes within the permafrost. Like a target with a bull's-eye surrounded by concentric circles, these units were organized more or less in latitudinal bands that radiated outward from the North Pole. The thicker and more continuous permafrost lay closest to the North Pole and grew thinner and more discontinuous as it approached the Arctic Circle.

Hinzman, Wullschleger, Wilson, and the rest of the team had chartered the plane to fly a path that cut a transect through the permafrost's five different ecoregions to pick locations to study, starting in the south and heading north. Along the way, they'd land at six airstrips in the middle of nowhere, built by the military in World War II and now used exclusively by hunters and prospectors. Wilson was stunned by the place's hard beauty. "It was fantastic. People live rough up here, but it will always hold a special place in my heart."

The NGEE Arctic team started their day outside the Native village of Council, in a drainage on the Seward Peninsula that sat on the permafrost's southernmost edge. The ground was hummocky and patchy. The tussock tundra was dry to the touch. Mosquitos swarmed. An encroaching black spruce forest was visible on the horizon, and a dense thicket of willows and alder shrubs was sprouting on the edges of a small flowing stream. In many places where the permafrost had recently thawed, the ground had collapsed into a sinkhole now filled with water and emerging plants. The area around Council had been frozen ground that climate change had already thawed. "This is what the future of the Arctic looks like," Hinzman told the scientists.

From Council, the scientists hopped aboard the plane and flew north, passing over permafrost transitioning from thawed or thawing on the southern extent to deeper, healthy, and intact frozen ground in the north. It became evident that, because of the sheer size of the land and the volume of questions they were hoping to answer, they needed to reduce the scope of the project to more manageable bites.

"Polygonal tundra," Wilson yelled to Hinzman over the engine several hours into the flight. She pointed toward the landscape sprawling out below. North of the Brooks Range, Alaska flattens into a broad coastal plain. The permafrost there has the honeycomb grid characteristic of one of the five types of permafrost. Called polygonal tundra, it looks like manicured farmland and makes up about 250,000 square kilometers, or 3 percent, of the entire Arctic landmass. Up until about twenty years ago, how polygonal tundra formed was utterly mysterious. Then scientists modeled the northern coastal plane's typical freeze-thaw cycle, the same pattern that causes ice to form and then melt again farther south. When the ground froze in the Arctic winter, it condensed and cracks formed. When it thawed again in summer, meltwater flowed into the cracks and drained toward the permafrost below. When the meltwater hit the ice, it froze again. The scientists discovered that over tens of thousands of years this process of freezing and thawing formed wedges of ice that grew inside the cracks until some became elevated above the ground itself. Not unlike an infected splinter, the ground forced the ice wedges and the small amount of soil that had formed on top of them upward and out. Where these wedges touched, a polygonal shape formed that, depending on the particularities of the land, could be 10 meters across or 100.

Hinzman knew the polygonal tundra well. He also knew that ice wedge polygons were extremely rich in carbon, that they were grossly understudied, and that climate models predicted that, at the current rate of warming, the polygonal tundra was going to disappear. In a sense, the patchwork of polygons scrolling out below was the very reason for NGEE Arctic. The polygons weren't in global climate models and couldn't be until observational scientists understood the processes that drove the system's particularities. And what would happen to the climate if and when the polygons vanished? "All the ecosystems in the Arctic are shifting north," Hinzman says. "That this landscape is disappearing was the key result that convinced the DOE to fund the project."

He gave Wilson a knowing nod as the plane dipped toward the northern town of Utqiagvik, formerly Barrow as earlier noted, descending on a narrow airstrip perched along the shores of the momentarily calm Arctic Ocean. Seven years later, what the scientists learned on that desolate patch of frozen ground would bring Lathrop and Wilson to Nome.

4

"Did you put it in park, Emma?" Wilson asks Lathrop. On a cool and cloudy morning in August 2019, Wilson is sitting shotgun in a rented Ford F-150 out front of the storage unit in Nome where NGEE Arctic keeps its equipment. Lathrop nods yes, hops out, and vanishes into a dilapidated wood building to fetch a special shovel, one with a heavy handle and a narrow spade that makes it easier to dig in frozen ground.

"If you're doing fieldwork, you need access to logistics," Wilson explains, sipping her coffee and raising her chin toward the storage facility, its white paint curled with age. Logistics played a major role in why, after expanding beyond Barrow, NGEE Arctic chose Nome as a research location. When it comes to roads and infrastructure, Nome is metropolitan compared to the rest of the Seward Peninsula. Famous today as the final stop of the Iditarod, Nome is an outpost on the Bering Sea's black and wind-stripped beaches. It's less than two hundred miles west to Russia, and a few miles east all signs of civilization disappear into mountains and a treeless tundra with no discernible end.

The town itself is a misnomer by definition. Nome got its name when an early explorer misread the words "No Name" scrawled onto a map of the Seward Peninsula. After gold was discovered on a beach on the Seward in 1899, miners camped out on the unsheltered beaches for months while the town sprung up like a well-watered weed. Wood was shipped from the south and houses erected with little or no thought, the haphazard shacks, shanties, many bars, and miner supply posts spilling out onto the beaches. The town burned to the ground three times before residents replaced the wooden buildings with less flammable materials.

Anything that hasn't burned in Nome has never left. Century-old dredge miners built to syphon up permafrost and sift it for gold stand guard over mining ponds. Like steel dinosaurs, they're still the tallest buildings in town. At the dredge's feet, trucks of archaeological interest lay rusting in pits dug during William McKinley's presidency. Today, Nome claims two hotels, a bad Chinese restaurant, a slightly worse Chinese restaurant, a surprisingly good pho joint in a Vietnamese woman's dusty and cluttered living room, too many bars, and two grocery stores that both charge almost $10 a pound for asparagus and upwards of $20 for a six-pack of beer. There is also an airstrip that runs perpendicular to a salmon stream that, in the late August twilight, is lined with families fishing to fill their freezers.

This morning, with summer making its last gasps for the season, the day is seven minutes shorter than it had been the day before. At almost 9:00 a.m. the light is still that gauzy and golden quality of the north's famously long sunrises. Kids in camouflage pants are zipping up and down the town's mud streets on four wheelers, and it smells like two-stroke gasoline and sea salt.

"Compared to Barrow," Wilson laughs, "this is luxury."

UTQIAGVIK IS THE BIGGEST town on Alaska's North Slope and, for many of the same practical reasons that NGEE Arctic selected Nome as their base, where the team decided to start their field research. They work out of the Barrow Environmental Observatory, a research station built by the National Weather Service in the seventies that's about three kilometers south of the Arctic Ocean and about eight from town. It's basic. The living quarters, a simple hut, feature bunk beds, a galley kitchen, and a single small bathroom. "When we first came to Barrow to check it out for lodging, we immediately walked into the hut and said no way," Wilson remembers. Then they saw the town's other offerings and that hut won out. "We got to know each other pretty well," she says.

Within moments of landing in Utqiagvik on the last stop of their scouting flight, NGEE Arctic had picked it as the first research site. "Logistically, scientifically, it made great sense," says Wullschleger. Scientifically, the polygonal tundra represented a poorly understood ecoregion, but from a modeling perspective it also formed the northernmost type of permafrost. It gave the NGEE Arctic team a tidy solution: if they could expand their research from the polygonal tundra to the Seward Peninsula and the permafrost's southern extent, they could infer a gradient of change between the north and the south, multiplying the impact of their research.

With the location selected and a clear set of questions they hoped to answer, the task now became: How do we design our experiments so they tell us what we need to know? Called experimental design, this stage of research is one of Wilson's favorites. She is passionate about design and possesses an innate spatial intelligence that helps her visualize how landscapes form. "I have these visceral urges to create and build," she says. "I'm a visual person, a very spatial person."

At Barrow, Wilson acquainted herself with the existing research: What was already known about the hydrology of permafrost in general? What was known about the hydrology of the polygonal tundra specifically? And how did the models represent both? A literature review is standard practice for any scientist launching into any in-depth scientific endeavor. After dedicating a few months to surveying the known scientific world of polygonal tundra, Wilson then studied what the models were lacking.

Wilson enlisted the help of Christian Andreson, a post-doctoral student, to analyze how well global climate models with any representation of permafrost captured the range and variability of soil moisture across the landscape. Andreson compared a dozen models, starting each model before 1850, a year chosen because it's near the start of the industrial revolution and the beginning of humans' outsize impact on climate. The model used observed forcing data of the changing climate—wind, rain, snow, temperature, atmospheric CO_2 and greenhouse gases—to predict changes in the permafrost up to the present day and two hundred years into the future.

"It was eye-opening," Wilson recalls. Anderson's analysis found "huge, huge, variation in where things got wetter and drier and the spatial distributions of those trends," Wilson says. In other words, none of the models accurately reflected the observed distribution of soil moisture. One major shortcoming was that the models allowed water to flow vertically, meaning down into the soil column during rain events and then out of the soil column during evaporation. They do a poor job of representing how water moves through landscapes. In reality, Wilson and others hypothesized that meltwater moved not only vertically in the Arctic but also laterally in the soil itself when it hit the frost table, changing soil moisture and therefore emissions as it spread.

Wilson often says that water is "key to everything" in the Arctic, but in these models water's role was glossed over. The first step toward fixing that was figuring out how water actually moved in the tundra, which meant understanding how it moved differently in different *types* of the tundra. Having already divided the Arctic into landscape classifications, Wilson now needed to repeat the process at the much finer scale of the Utqiagvik research site: breaking the ground into classifications that were broadly represented of polygonal tundra. To do this, Wilson tapped into the high resolution satellite data collected over the area and hired an airplane to make a laser altimetry map, a sort of high-resolution image of the research site's topography. "That was pretty cool," Wilson says. "It leaves you with an extremely fine-scale representation of the landscape."

To the untrained eye, from a plane or a satellite, the polygonal tundra all looked nearly identical. In fact, the map revealed four main types of ice wedge polygons: those with a high center; those with a low center that were mostly filled with water; those with a flat center; and those with a low center that were degrading. Four landscape classes, each containing different volumes of carbon and different types of soil, were all located within a kilometer of each other at the

Barrow site. Wilson could measure, in detail, one polygon from each class and use that information to infer how all the others might behave across the entire Arctic. It became immediately evident to Wilson and the NGEE Arctic team that this partitioning of the landscape would be valuable for more than just her research.

"This is how we should structure all of our experimental design," Wilson argued when the entire NGEE Arctic team met on a conference call a couple months later. "We should colocate our research using this strategy." Wilson's case was that the best approach to unlocking the Arctic was to stay the course: divide the landscape into representative classes, then have everybody look deep into each of those different classes. The group agreed. The tactic would inform the larger NGEE Arctic plan: where to install towers that sniffed methane and CO_2 emissions; the micro–weather stations that quantified air movement at the scale of a human palm; and instruments to continuously measure how both water and heat moved through the soil, monitor solar radiation fluxes, and perform hundreds of other procedures. All of which would vastly improve the models of global climate. "We had this idea of fantastic overlapping data sets that nobody else in the community had because most people didn't design their research that way." Wilson says.

All of this work occurred with nothing more than a loose

understanding that the Department of Energy was interested in funding NGEE Arctic's studies. Securing the grant required steady work for years from each of ten different scientists just to generate the proposal. In 2011, a month and a half after Wilson first visited Utqiagvik and a few weeks after submitting the final 192-page proposal, the DOE rewarded Wullschleger, Wilson, and the others' efforts. They were awarded $27,000,000 through 2014.

SCIENTISTS OFTEN FALL INTO two categories: lumpers and splitters. Splitters try to tease apart all the world's variability, diving deep into individual processes or organisms and finding everything they can about how these work. Lumpers try to define where that variability is most relevant so they can "lump" similarities together into larger groups. Wilson insists she is neither.

"I'm indifferent about lumping and splitting. You have to figure out how to use each in an economical way," Wilson says. "For this project we're trying to do the splitting in a meaningful way so we can tell the global modelers how to split. But, really, what we're doing is trying to figure out the best way to do the lumping."

The equipment necessary to give the modelers those instructions is cumbersome. Wilson estimated the instrumentation needed for NGEE Arctic to take their measurements at Barrow alone weighed three tons. For most of 2012, the year after the proposal was accepted by the DOE, each scientist organized equipment, found and ordered existing instruments, or just invented new things. Wilson ordered from a logging supply company three-foot-long thermometers designed to take the internal temperature of hay bales and used them to measure active layer depth. "Scientists get very creative," she says with a shrug.

That first summer Wilson and her team lugged tons of gear into the soggy tundra. At first they slung the stuff over their shoulders and used tightropes to cross the raised platforms the research teams had built over the polygons, climbing down only in the final stages to set up the instruments in soggy ground. They tried using wheelbarrows to lighten the loads, but it was too hard to push them in the tussocks. Then one technician, a hunter, recommended they use a game cart like the one he used to transport elk carcasses out of the wilderness. The team ordered one, flew it to Barrow, and used it to shuttle three-hundred-pound loads of gear to the research site. Moving gear in the winter offered its own unique set of challenges. Temperatures could be -20°F, with winds of 25 miles per hour, and there were moments when the winds kicked up loose snow and the world went completely white, blinding the researchers. Wilson weathered those conditions while on a snowmobile, swaddled in dozens of pounds of clothing and skipping across the frozen world. "That's when I got my nickname, 'Full Throttle,'" she says proudly.

For the next three years, a rotating cast of scientists flew in and out of Utqiagvik to collect measurements. The data sets they compiled were novel and rich in details—on the enzymes that determined the photosynthesis rates of arctic plants; on the peculiar hydrology of ice wedge polygons; on micro topography's influence on snow depth and distribution—but it would take the scientists another three years to sort out all of that information.

By 2019 they had sifted through much of it. In total, NGEE Arctic researchers would publish more than two hundred scientific papers—a trove—on Utqiagvik and polygonal tundra alone. Some of these papers focused narrowly on the splits: detailing the exact process of carbon leaching from high-center polygons into the atmosphere. Others were papers of lumped ideas: how a collection of various low- and high-center polygons drains and how their drying across large expanses of the Arctic is impacting global climate. The short answer, unsurprisingly, is that it's complicated. But the upshot is that rapid change is not good for global climate no matter how you slice it. The drying polygons are dumping more CO_2 into the atmosphere, accelerating climate change. In places where the landscape is getting wetter, the polygons are dumping more methane, or CH_4, into the atmosphere, accelerating climate change even further.

Most importantly, for Wullschleger and Wilson, the resounding and early success of NGEE Arctic's research in Barrow convinced the Department of Energy that they were capable of organizing and conducting first-class research in extreme environments. In 2015 the DOE signed up for a second phase of NGEE Arctic, committing to three more years of data collection and analysis that would expand the project to an entirely new research site—preferably one that would represent a different ecoregion of permafrost. Wullschleger and Wilson already had a good idea where this would be. They wanted to go to the opposite end of the permafrost spectrum, away from hardy permafrost found in the polygonal tundra and toward the south, where the permafrost was already beginning to thaw: Nome. By bookending the Arctic's permafrost, the thinking went, they could capture a gradient of conditions in between.

"We knew we were going to have to completely redo things in the Seward," Wilson says. And this time it would be exponentially more complicated. In Utqiagvik they had measured four different classes of polygons, landscape features that were no larger than 200 feet across and never more than a short walk from each other. To understand how the thawing permafrost worked around Nome, they would have to measure watersheds that spanned miles and that would require three-hour drives or helicopter flights to reach.

AFTER PICKING UP THE shovel from the storage shed, Lathrop and Wilson head east in the F-150 to catch a dirt road to Kougarok. A caravan of salmon fishermen in Polaris RZRs (pronounced "razors"), covered four-wheelers popular among rural Alaskans, whine past, the camo-clad men inside tossing two-fingered waves at the scientists. The road heads inland, tracing a broad coastal river before squeezing through a string of spectacular peaks. In the late morning light, the mountains look naked. The only plants on them are the iconic high and tawny grassy tussocks. Filling the valleys are willows and alders just tall enough to hide bull moose and grizzly bears. But although the land is sparsely populated now, only geologic time can erase the imprint miners left on the Seward Peninsula. Around each corner seems to appear another rickety flume or an exposed hillside blasted to rubble. Like open wounds, these slopes look like they'll never heal. If the landscape surrounding Barrow was defined by sameness, the Seward Peninsula is defined by its Arctic diversity.

"Oh, this is nothing," Wilson says of a vista befitting a David Attenborough narration. "It's getting even prettier."

"This is my favorite drive out here," Lathrop adds.

The same qualities that make the Seward so visually striking also make it much harder to study. The terrain is steep and mountainous. There are massive rivers, lakes, and watersheds vegetated with woody plants that up until recently were far less prevalent on the Seward. The diversity and landscape and apparent changes prompted a number of questions. How fast was the land already changing? Where did the water drain during the snowmelt and storm events? Where did it puddle? What were the effects on the surface and subsurface? Why did the shrubs grow in some places but not others? Where did the carbon collect? If the permafrost thawed in the flatlands, would the ground collapse like Swiss cheese? If it thawed on the hill slopes, would it slough like melted ice cream?

All of these factors interacted to create the change that Seward natives intuitively understood even if they didn't use the phrase "climate change." They knew that moose hunting season no longer coincided with the animal's historic migration. Last year they plowed through a snowpack deeper than at any other point in history. They breathed smoke from Arctic wildfires unheard-of until recently, and spent hours in line waiting for construction equipment to fix roads destroyed by anomalous spring rains. The polar regions are often called the canary in the coal mine for climate change. The locals were living through it.

In 2016, when NGEE Arctic shifted its focus to the Seward Peninsula, Wilson took the lead on designing the experimental sites. The peninsula spans more than 20,600 square miles of widely varied geography. To slice it up, Wilson and the NGEE team applied the same clustering process they'd used in Barrow to lump and split the land into coherent pieces. The terrain was far too complex to capture within a single intensive research site, as they'd done in Barrow. Instead, they'd have to fan out into the three major classifications of permafrost conditions she identified on the peninsula: the hilly permafrost near the Bering Sea, the more continuous permafrost inland, and the rapidly thawing permafrost on the peninsula and the Arctic's southern boundary. Within each of these bands, the team found watersheds that offered a close approximation of the whole range of environmental conditions on the Seward Peninsula. Within each of the three selected sites, Wilson and the NGEE Arctic team zoomed in again. (This practice of zooming in and out to select representative sites is essential to translating observational climate science into global models.)

"In the Seward, each watershed required the same amount of work as we'd put into just the Barrow site, and we even underestimated how hard that research would be," Bolton says. "In Barrow, the variability wasn't as obvious at first, but the more we zoomed in, the more we learned that micro-topography is every bit as complex as macro-topography. On the Seward, we had both micro- and macro-topography. It was just harder."

Once Wilson and the NGEE Arctic team had picked three sites within the Seward Peninsula, she ran transects through the watersheds. In one area, she crosshatched a tic-tac-toe pattern across the slope with multiple transects running down the hill and two running across it like contour lines. At other sites she picked transects that were scattered across the slopes or aspects with apparent whimsy—a ridge or rocky outcrop here, a bog or alder thicket there—but, in truth, each transect was selected with hyper-specificity and intentionality. Taken together, these suites of transects operated like telescopes. By starting wide and then zooming in, they were trying to account for as much variability as the peninsula had to offer. Wilson was both lumping and splitting.

To help with the last critical piece of scaling their work to the pan-Arctic, Wilson and Bolton forged a partnership with NASA. As part of the scientific gold rush in the Arctic, the space organization had launched a remote sensing campaign earlier in the decade. Their work hinged upon flying over the Arctic in planes rigged with tons of scientific equipment, but the campaign lacked the intensive ground research that NGEE Arctic offered. Wilson and Bolton proposed that the organizations collaborate. The idea was that NASA would fly overhead on the exact day that Wilson and her team were collecting soil moisture measurements in the field: the researchers on the ground would corroborate the data that the airplanes and satellites collected from above. And if what NASA saw from the air or from space was wrong, they could fix it.

"One of the coolest collaborations I've ever set up," Wilson says. "It was such a wonderful collaborative plan."

Unfortunately, in climate science, even the best-laid plans often fail.

5

——

It's a cool and damp coastal evening, and after a long day of measuring permafrost depths at Kougarok, Bolton, Wilson, Lathrop, and Jin are recovering in the team's apartment. The tidy nine-hundred-square foot apartment that NGEE Arctic rents out for its scientists sits a couple blocks from the finish line of the Iditarod. The place is painted a pastel yellow, a colorful tactic common in the northern latitudes. Out in front of the house next door is a late-seventies pickup with two flat tires. A pair of damp polar bear hides are draped across the hood, and three huskies are chained to the trailer hitch. Up the street, a small herd of musk oxen, probably pushed out of the wilderness by a grizzly bear, are milling about in the grass in the cemetery. The town is quiet.

The apartment is warm and muggy with a coatrack adorned with pants and jackets—all Eddie Bauer, Patagonia, and other high-quality brands—while the *Nome Nugget*, the oldest continuously printed newspaper in Alaska, sits open on the kitchen table to a story in the designated "Climate Watch" section. It's about how unseasonably warm sea temperatures are hurting this year's salmon fishing and crab harvest.

"Did you read your email today, Cathy?" Bolton asks. He's sitting on the couch, scanning his in-box on his laptop while taking his time with a beer.

"No, I haven't been able to download," Wilson says. She's sitting next to him, wrapped in her blue Patagonia puffy jacket and waiting patiently for the team to head out for dinner. Tonight it's Milano's Pizzeria, a restaurant in the basement of a historic gold mining hotel that sells everything from Korean food to spaghetti. ("Nome has edible food," says Wilson, reaching for her highest compliment on the town's dining opportunities.)

"We've got a conversation ahead of us tonight," Bolton warns. "The plane broke down and may not leave Montana for two weeks," he says.

"My God," Wilsons gasps. That plane was the Grumman Gulfstream II, or G-II, the workhorse of NASA's ABoVE (Arctic-Boreal Vulnerability Experiment) field campaign, the sister experiment to NGEE Arctic. The flight was a necessary step toward measuring soil moisture from space, the linchpin in the Seward Peninsula project. On board the G-II was an instrument called a synthetic aperture radar (SAR) that, as Wilson explained later, sent out electromagnetic waves and measured how long it took them to return to the instrument. This information would serve a proxy for soil moisture. If it worked, instead of spending two weeks collecting soil moistures from a few hundred different points in a few watersheds, they could look at the soil moisture of the entire Arctic from satellites. Except that now the flight wasn't happening.

"This is just part of climate science," Wilson says, clearly frustrated. She gets up from her spot on the couch and paces a bit, setting her beer down on the living room table before speaking quietly to herself. "We'll make something work."

For a detail-oriented personality who prefers to control all that she can, learning to deal with the innate uncertainty of climate science came as a challenge. Wilson was born in Jacksonville, Florida, in 1955, a year when the carbon dioxide content in the atmosphere was still at a comfortable 315 parts per million (100 parts per million less than it is now) and climate change, let alone a career in the field, was a concept as alien as iPhones.

Wilson's father, Robert Darrell Wilson, had grown up in the Pacific Northwest the son of a traveling logger. When he was a teenager, a family friend recognized Bob's keen intelligence and helped him get into college. He studied engineering at Oregon State University until World War II began and he was sent to the Pacific theater. With the Seabees, he built infrastructure while island-hopping behind the Marines north toward Japan. One of his last missions was assessing the damage in Nagasaki. He flew over the destroyed city shortly after the United States dropped the atomic bomb—a weapon built on the same New Mexico mesa where his daughter would eventually spend the best years of her career.

After the war, Bob finished a degree in architecture and moved to Washington, D.C., where he met his wife, Helen Anne "Lynne" Wilson, who was working for the State Department. Soon after, Bob built a distinguished career as a campus architect. Over the next twenty years the family would move four times between California, Connecticut, and Michigan. Cathy Wilson says that her father was driven and highly ethical, demanding high-quality work and refining projects until he'd created the final product he'd first envisioned—a doggedness Wilson would inherit.

From an early age, the gifts that would eventually propel Cathy Wilson's career were readily apparent. As early as the sixth grade, a teacher recognized her aptitude in math, the foundation of modeling. "Mr. Cross," Wilson recalls, wistfully. "He didn't treat me like a little kid, but, like, he expected me to perform up to my potential and do things properly." In a note on her report card, Mr. Cross said Wilson should be encouraged to pursue mathematics. A similar thing happened with Mr. Law, who taught geometry in high school, after Wilson pulled down the highest marks he'd ever given in the class.

Curious about everything and thrilled by well-told stories, Wilson was then, as she is now, a voracious reader. By high school she was devouring Hermann Hesse, Kurt Vonnegut, and Carlos Castaneda. By then the family had moved to Connecticut and Wilson was playing the part of a California hippie in intricately self-embroidered jeans and a leotard, a free spirit among friends that she called preppies. She was a good enough student but not outstanding. "Top marks in the classes I loved, and Bs or passing in those I didn't," she shrugs. She was in high school during the peak of the civil rights movement, the anti-war protests, and a nationwide awakening to environmentalism. In an age of social strife, Wilson began to see herself as both an environmental and social activist, a person who created change by throwing her weight and intellect behind an issue. Several times she took trips to Washington to protest the Vietnam War, and in 1970 she organized a march of several hundred students on the inaugural Earth Day.

"She danced to the beat of her own drum," is how her mother likes to describe Cathy. As with many teenagers, the tension between mother and daughter was ever present. "I was incredibly willful and self-centered. I was going to do what I set out to do and I was going to do it the way I wanted to," Wilson recalls, acknowledging her role in a long-ago head-butting. (Wilson notes that today her relationship with her mom is excellent: they are closer than they've ever been). But she attributes some of that tension to a changing age. Despite a promising early career as a secretary in the State Department, Lynne gave up that path to become a stay-at-home mom looking after four children. Wilson says her mother, as many smart and capable women did then, felt trapped by her generation's ideas of a woman's responsibilities. By the late 1960s, women's rights were becoming more on a par with men's, and Wilson, who was out protesting wars and playing Bob Dylan too loud, was riding a wave of opportunities unavailable to her mother. But as she would learn cruelly in the coming years, many men still felt there should still be hard limits imposed on a woman's career.

After Wilson graduated high school in 1973, she went to Mills College, a women's liberal arts school in Oakland. Her dad's job as campus architect allowed for a tuition exchange that made the pricey education affordable for the solidly middle-class family. At Mills, Wilson didn't know what she wanted to do with her life, but she discovered an unlikely passion for theater arts: not acting or dancing but building and designing—skills that would serve her well in climate science decades later. "I loved hanging studio lights and actually getting my hands dirty constructing the sets," she remembers.

She picked fine arts as her major. But at Mills she could also take classes that were outside of her major's requirements, a small perk that directed her life's course. In the spring of her sophomore year she took calculus from a well-known professor, Lorene Blum, who also taught at Berkeley. Sitting in the front row of Blum's classes, Wilson felt that the passion with which Blum taught math reminded her of her own love for the subject. She found the logic and clarity of numbers titillating and latched on to the idea that, when properly organized, formulas could describe any process in life. "Math is the language of God," Wilson remembers, paraphrasing a famous Galileo quote, "Mathematics is the language in which God has written the universe," after a series of stirring lectures on derivatives. Shortly after, she switched her major to math.

The fall of 1974, Wilson's dad accepted a job as the campus planner at the University of Michigan in Flint. With his new appointment, the tuition exchange that Wilson needed to afford Mills College vanished. "You can keep going to school at Michigan," her dad told her. With little money and fewer options, Wilson left Northern California and moved to Ann Arbor, where she took classes at the University of Michigan as the only woman in their math department. Michigan was frigid in the winter and damp in the spring and summer compared to the Bay Area, and she soon fell into a deep depression. "I was very, very lonely," Wilson says.

Wilson finished out her junior year, winning honors in the math department, and then dropped out and took a job tending bar. Several months later, when she was still spinning her wheels, the secretary at her dad's office mentioned that the Fisher Body Company plant in nearby Grand Blanc was hiring. During World War II the company had built the Sherman tank. Now they took raw metal and, using machine presses—which could crush and had crushed workers' arms—stamped the panels for all of General Motors' vehicles. "They're hiring," the secretary told Wilson one day.

She started in the press room. There, in a line of seven factory workers in a cacophony of clanging metal, Wilson hefted sheets of steel cut off metal rolls and weighing hundreds of tons. She slung them through a series of huge die cutters that stamped them into the shapes of doors, tailgates, side panels, and hoods. "I really enjoyed it at first," she remembers. Using a trick that would serve her later, she made the work a game: race the other workers. "Could I beat the guy to my left? To my right? Could I do it with some style?" she says, smiling at the memory and pantomiming the motions of a job forty years in her past.

Within a few months of getting the job, Wilson was put in charge of a line, setting the pace for others to follow. Six months after that, her foreman pulled her aside and asked if she'd be interested in being one of two women selected to be the factory's first female supervisors. "It was kind of thrilling," Wilson recalls. "I'd found success where I didn't really expect to find it at all." Her introduction to management was far rougher than any other challenge she'd face over the rest of her career.

"This is a hard thing to remember," Wilson says, wiping tears from her eyes. She went to foreman school for a week. But instead of supervising her fellow employees stamping metal, she was put in charge of the team loading finished pallets of car parts to be shipped all over the United States and Mexico. All of her workers were male, and none had ever had a female boss, let alone one who was, in some cases, twenty years their junior. The men challenged her authority every chance they could. They disappeared during shifts, said they couldn't find parts that were in stock in the warehouse, or intentionally dawdled on the job. "Their defiance had only one purpose: to make me feel inferior," Wilson says. "They wanted me to quit."

At the time, she didn't have a managerial tool kit, so she made one. She tried leading by example, then reasoning, pleading, and badgering. Eventually, Wilson created a series of disciplinary actions that started with a call to the men's union reps and ended with a week of no pay. If the men didn't shape up after that, she went to her superiors. Unmoved, the men adopted guerrilla tactics to intimidate her. They spray-painted crude messages about her on the sides of box-cars that traveled the country's rails. They slashed the tires on her car. She says that one once tried to run her over with a forklift and another threatened to kill her. Wilson's depression deepened. Still, she didn't quit. She needed the money, she rationalized. But she stayed for a bigger reason: "It was determination. I'd never been in a situation where people were out to get me. Literally out to get me. But I wasn't going to let them," she states. She never broke and "nothing has been harder since," she says. Eventually the men started toe-ing the line.

After a year and half in the job, the plant manager called her into his office for her performance assessment. "We think you could be the first female plant manager," he told her. Wilson, who even then was well-dressed in slacks and a tie, because "that's what the male supervisor wore," remembers the swell of pride she felt: to win in an environment where her coworkers thought she didn't belong. Wilson shook her boss's hand and, on a cold November day, walked out of his office past the men loading quarter panels onto boxcars. She paused for a moment and watched them work. *What the hell am I doing here?* she thought. Having proven to herself that she had the grit to stick to anything while also gaining significant managerial experience, Wilson's mind once again returned to math.

6

Charles David Keeling wasn't the godfather of climate science. Nobody is. But he did more to make the science relevant than anybody before or since. It was the mid-fifties, about two hundred years since humans figured out that burning coal, oil, and other fossil fuels could power the industrial revolution. Keeling, who would soon discover that burning fossil fuels was warming the world, was a scientific nobody. He was a postdoctoral student at CalTech, in Pasadena, California, and transfixed by a debate raging among meteorologists: Was the carbon dioxide released by burning fossil fuels changing the chemical composition of the atmosphere?

The idea that the atmosphere contained invisible materials that kept the world warm was an old one. In the 1820s the French mathematician and physicist Joseph Fourier calculated that given the amount of sun that reaches the earth each day, our world should be a lot cooler than it is. He proposed an idea, later proven correct, that the atmosphere acts like a blanket. When sunlight enters the atmosphere, about a third of it hits clouds or light spots on the earth—like snow or deserts—and is reflected back into space. But, like sunlight on a black T-shirt, when rays hit the earth's dark spots—trees, dirt, rock—the warmth gets absorbed, and the earth radiates heat back into the atmosphere in the form of longwave radiation. A percentage of that radiation is then absorbed by carbon dioxide molecules or other greenhouse gases in the atmosphere; these molecules act like bricks in a fireplace by staying warm long after the fire is extinguished. Called the natural greenhouse effect, all that invisible matter keeps global temperatures stable. The greenhouse effect is the reason there is life on our planet. Without it, the temperature of the earth would be −22°F (−30°C).

When Keeling started studying climatology, the field was a dull scientific backwater devoted mainly to compiling statistics from routine weather observations, such as average temperature or precipitation volumes. The debate over carbon dioxide's role in global temperature was the field's lone flashpoint. One side argued that the earth's plants, which process CO_2 during photosynthesis, and oceans, which absorb CO_2, would simply remove whatever extra CO_2 manmade devices pumped into the atmosphere. Another widely held position was that the extra CO_2 might lead to a small increase in global temperatures. A third, significantly smaller group aligned with Guy Stewart Callendar, a British engineer who had calculated by hand that rising CO_2 concentrations would warm the globe significantly. It wouldn't be until the end of the twentieth century, long after Callendar's death, that climatology's leading authorities recognized his stroke of genius. But confirming Callendar's theory required its own stroke of genius: recording an accurate measure of CO_2 concentrations in the atmosphere.

That was Keeling's gift to science. Back in the fifties, Keeling developed a gas manometer, an instrument that could measure CO_2 in the air and water. A lover of the outdoors, he loaded the instrument, his wife, and his infant son into the car and drove Highway 101 south to Big Sur, a remote beach about two hours south of the Bay Area. He picked the site because, he reasoned, it had to be far removed from the localized influence of urban pollutants. For three weeks Keeling and his young family camped on a beach in the shade of redwoods. He took samples every day and night, a process that he then repeated months later when collecting a similar group of samples in the rain forests of Washington's Olympic Peninsula and the desert of Arizona's mountains. The data told the same story. At distinct locations separated by nearly five hundred miles, the average concentration of carbon in the air was 310 parts per million (ppm). These were single data points in time and space that didn't indicate whether that number was relatively high, relatively low, or changing. But Keeling had done what nobody else had: he'd derived an accurate measurement of atmospheric CO_2 concentrations and demonstrated that the gas was distributed relatively evenly throughout the atmosphere. Now he had to figure out what, if anything, that meant.

In 1958, shortly after Keeling published his findings, the U.S. Weather Bureau, predecessor of the National Oceanic and Atmospheric Administration (NOAA), hired Keeling to run their continuous CO_2 monitoring program. With government support and money, Keeling installed his first ground-based instrument on a barren patch of cooled lava 12,000 feet up the slopes of Hawaii's Mauna Loa, an active volcano far removed from industry. Temperate, isolated, devoid of nearby plants that might breathe any extra carbon, this was an optimal location for continuously measuring atmospheric carbon dioxide.

After sixty-two years of continuous measurements, the graph Keeling's instruments continuously add to is known as the Keeling Curve. It looks like an EKG reading from a healthy patient climbing a staircase. In the summer, when the earth's plants grow and take in CO_2, its atmospheric levels dip. In the winter, when the plants lose their leaves, the CO_2 levels in the atmosphere rise again. Keeling had measured earth's breathing cycle. But it took a few years of measurements before the graph's gravity became clear. "Where data extend beyond one year, averages for the second year are higher than for the first year. . . . At the South Pole the observed rate of increase is nearly that to be expected from the combustion of fossil fuel," he wrote (*The Warming Papers*, Oxford, UK: Wiley, 2011). In plain language, Keeling's measurements showed that the earth was breathing as it always had. But neither plants nor the ocean were going to absorb the extra CO_2 that was releasing into the atmosphere as a consequence of burning fossil fuel. Atmospheric CO_2 was skyrocketing. Now the question became: How would this extra CO_2 affect global climate?

CLIMATE IS AVERAGE WEATHER over time, and people have always cared about weather. Within fifty years of the thermometer's invention in the early 1600s, weather collection networks sprouted in Italy. By the middle of the nineteenth century, they'd spread everywhere in the world where people lived. Charles Keeling's work simply demonstrated that human activity was changing the climate.

"The remaining scientific task, to learn all about the implications of climate change, is enormous and incomplete, but in one sense it is just filling in the details," says Richard Somerville, a climate scientist and professor at Scripps

Institution of Oceanography of the University of California, San Diego, where Keeling spent much of his later career. "Therefore, all current work on climate change references the Keeling Curve, either explicitly or tacitly. 'Epochal' is the term I prefer when describing the importance of his work."

Keeling's findings prompted a scientific revolution. Before his discovery, climate science lay largely in the realm of meteorology. Subsequently, climate science left the atmosphere to enter nearly every geoscience and even some biological and social ones; scientific knowledge about global climate and the processes that drive it has been leap-frogging itself ever since. The number of papers on climate science has increased exponentially, doubling about every eleven years: 95 percent of the scientific literature on the topic was published after 1951. The questions scientists were racing to answer in the mid-twentieth century were global and spanned the earth's history. To know where the climate was going, they first had to know where it had been.

In the 1960s and '70s, researchers started making pilgrimages to Antarctica and Greenland's ice sheet, where a record of time lay frozen in ancient ice. Like strata in geology, the oldest layers of ice were situated near the bottom of the ice sheet and contained microscopic bubbles of air locked in the frozen water: carbon from past atmospheres. By borrowing drills designed for oil extraction technologies, researchers used increasingly large drills to bore holes almost two miles deep into the ice sheets. By sampling the carbon concentrations of those deepest air bubbles and at increments through the gradient above, paleoclimatologists constructed a history of CO_2 concentrations that dates back 800,000 years. They found that 10,000 years before the industrial revolution there were 280 parts of carbon per million in the ice. (It was 315 ppm when Keeling first measured, and it's 415 ppm now.) They measured the atmosphere and saw how carbon concentrations correlated to ice ages and warmer periods; they were able to determine that, without question, climate and atmospheric CO_2 concentrations were inseparably linked. But as important as it was, was it the only driver of global climate?

As ice researchers compiled a record of historic CO_2, our understanding of nature's interconnectedness and how it affected climate grew. Teams of scientists began drilling cores from sediment layers in the ocean floor to understand how the oceans were cycling carbon. Others were conducting studies in Europe's glaciers to reveal changes in regional climate. There were studies of photosynthesis rates of different plant species in the Amazon's rain forest, of cactuses in the Kalahari Desert, and of bristlecone pines in mountains of Nevada. Sure, all plants chemically scrubbed carbon from the atmosphere through photosynthesis. But did some species photosynthesize faster than others? Yes. A plant's age mattered tremendously, as did where it lived, when it grew, and what soils it grew in. To understand carbon uptake rates required knowing the particularities of individual plant species and how those species changed with the seasons. The complexity kept expanding, and no aspect of the earth's climate record was too small to study.

Scientists learned that oceans did indeed process carbon, but new studies showed uptake rates depended on circulation patterns from the surface to the deep ocean. The findings gave both scientists and climate skeptics a hard shock. The ocean processes carbon much slower than anybody anticipated. Later studies showed that whales and dolphins moving from the ocean surface to great depths also played a role in mixing carbon. Scientists outfitted instruments on Japanese merchant vessels to sample sea surface temperatures, and in 1966 the Nimbus-2, the first satellite launched specifically to investigate global climate, was shot into space. Nimbus would last just three years before its hardware failed, but it marked the start of remote sensing, a tool that scientists would come to rely on for validating climate models.

Our understanding of climate complexity deepened. Methane, ozone, and brown and black carbon were all added to the list of greenhouse gases. Veerabhadran Ramanathan, now a professor at Scripps, thought to investigate what chlorofluorocarbons, chemicals used in refrigerants, did to the atmosphere. He had worked as an engineer in an Indian refrigeration company in his youth and knew chlorofluorocarbons had the potential to leak from the refrigerators' closed systems. He found that once chlorofluorocarbons reach the atmosphere, they're 10,000 times more potent as greenhouse gas than carbon dioxide.

As the field of climate research expanded, so did its monitoring networks. Today, more than 400 million weather stations update land surface temperatures in real time, and more than 4 million do the same for the sea. The National Weather Service alone collects 6.3 billion observations per day. But observational science can only take the pulse of the current global climate. "The measurements can tell you what's out there, but they don't tell you what's driving it," says Michael J. Prather, a professor and modeler at the University of California, Irvine, and one of the lead authors of a recent IPCC report, which issues authoritative reports on the state of the earth's climate every six to seven years. "Only models that represented how earth system processes *interact* to create climate could do that," he says.

In the early twentieth century, the idea that humans could use math to represent the earth's weather—and predict what it would be like one hundred years into the future—was ambitious, but scientists didn't shy from the idea. In 1922 the English mathematician and meteorologist Lewis Richardson imagined using differential equations to forecast weather. He envisioned breaking the world up into a grid of cells and packing those cells with functions and equations that all interacted with each other to solve what the weather would be at one point on the planet at one time. It was exactly what climate models would eventually do. The problem was that, in 1922, Fry estimated that to create an eight-hour weather forecast for England he would need 64,000 human calculators working nonstop for six weeks. He even made a plan for how to do this: pack all those number crunchers into a single stadium.

It would take until the mid-1950s before anybody actually tried to work out the complex math. The first general circulation model, as the predecessor to global climate models was known, was fast for its time. It used 5,000kb of memory—enough to store about four seconds of a modern MP3—to create a seasonal weather pattern that looked vaguely similar to earth's. By today's standards it was simple, and could only predict where and when summer and winter would fall for different parts of the globe. But it was a thrilling glimpse at what models could do. Like a fuzzy crystal ball, they could assemble observed science and predict a future world—something that, even if it wasn't exactly true to reality, showed the range of possibilities that might come to earth. Models were alternative realities, and alternate realities could teach scientists a great deal about our own.

From the 1950s onward, while the giants of observational research used ice cores and sediment drills to extend science's understanding of climatic drivers, modelers got busy making a chain of digital knots that, one small, painstaking piece of data at a time, would eventually link together all of the earth's systems.

The modeler Syukuro Manabe contributed more to this moonshot-like effort than most. In 1965 he wrote one of the most-cited climate science papers of all time. It was an elegant physics solution: a one-dimensional model that predicted with astounding clarity what would happen if humans kept pumping CO_2 into the atmosphere. Based on Keeling's findings, Manabe doubled the concentration. The model predicted the climate would warm between 4°F and 6°F, exactly within the range that current models show.

From there, Manabe kept adding complexity. Two years later, he and an oceanographer at NOAA's Geophysical Fluid Dynamics Laboratory in Princeton built a model that showed circulation patterns in the ocean. Two years after that, they coupled that model to an atmospheric model to represent how ice, sea, and air interacted to create climate. By 1975, Manabe had constructed something that began to look like a modern global climate model. It ran equations to represent the earth's radiation and solar flux, the uptake of carbon by the world's forests and oceans, fluid dynamics of clouds, and hundreds of other processes. It had an atmosphere, an ocean, and topography, with a grid size of 500 kilometers by 500 kilometers (about 311 by 311 miles), and if you closed one eye and spun around a few times, it even started to look like the earth.

By the late 1970s, climate change was appearing on world leaders' radars and moving beyond academia. Flush with money from the ongoing space race with the Soviet Union, NASA was also investing in the far less competitive race to build an accurate global climate model. Leading their team was James Hansen, a NASA modeler who became internationally famous in 1988 for testifying before Congress that the age of global warming had arrived. At the time he was the lead climate scientist in an office filled with computers the size of mini-fridges. He and his team were tinkering with the technology, trying to squeeze a code that represented the entire earth's climate onto a 3-inch-by-3-inch floppy disk.

"Manabe and Hansen were just trying to keep the science going. They were building these models because they wanted to know if they could write code that accurately represented fluid dynamics. Are we doing radiation right? How does the climate respond in the model if we ratchet up CO_2?" says Prather, the IPCC modeler. "Sure, they wanted to answer the question of what CO_2 would do to global climate, but there was no national imperative to understand climate change."

The national imperative came in 1979, after more scientific work, largely in the realm of academia, revealed that climate change was fast becoming an issue of global importance. That year the director of the Office of Science and the president of the National Academy of Science asked Jule Gregory Charney, director of MIT's Atmospheric and Ocean Dynamics Project, to chair a team of thirteen scientists and modelers representing the country's top research institutions. Their mission was to determine just how likely it was that the extra CO_2 would warm the globe.

Charney's team would produce what would become known as the Charney Report. In it, they'd used the world's top global climate models (GCMs)—Hansen and Manabe's among them—to predict what would happen if you doubled the amount of CO_2 in the atmosphere. This overlapping technique, where a conclusion is based on the consensus finding of multiple different models, was the predecessor of today's IPCC reports that are now the standard of global climate forecasting. Although the precise outcome of global climate is always unpredictable, Charney's report assumed that the most likely outcome lay somewhere within the range of conditions that the world's most skillful climate models provided. The report's predictions were exactly what

Manabe had said years earlier: climate change was coming. The public had its first clear theoretical warning. The disasters would soon follow.

SINCE THE CHARNEY REPORT, the models have only become better at predicting exactly how climate change plays out. Early GCMs gave linear predictions, showing how climate would respond to whatever variable was changed: solar radiation, carbon dioxide, total area of forests. They were smooth lines when in reality global climate is chaos—dynamic, variable, sensitive in the extreme to certain changes, and seemingly numb to others. "The biggest problem is that even with the same external forcing and boundary conditions, you get different results. The earth's current climatic condition is just one expression of any thousands that could have played out," Prather points out. "The variability in the earth's climate is real. We had to develop a model that could capture the range of possibility."

It was well into the 1990s before computers became powerful enough to capture larger ranges of possibility, and they've only improved since. Today's computers are a trillion times faster than the computers running Hansen's first models. "No single person knows what is a global climate model anymore," Prather observes. "They are way too big for that." They can solve 14 trillion calculations per second and run through a ream of code that would span 18,000 pages if printed out. Arriving at this point has taken the careers of tens of thousands of scientists and coders.

"We want to know: What happens to these emergent properties when we kick the system?" says Gavin A. Schmidt, the director of NASA's Goddard Institute for Space Studies. "There are wobbles in the earth's orbit that change the climate. There are changes in the solar cycles every eleven years that change the climate. Big volcanoes go off. Changes in biomass burning, in smoke, in aerosols. The ozone hole, deforestation, contrails, and greenhouse gases change the climate," Today's models incorporate all this. Now, Schmidt says, climate scientists are narrowing the scope, getting into increasingly finer-scale processes to improve the accuracy of the model runs. But then, he says, there remain a few poorly understood regions in the world with tremendous implications for global climate.

"That one would eat an axle," Wilson says of one of many potholes as she drives the Ford F-150 along a dirt road near the coast. It's a few days after she and the team heard the news about the cancelled NASA flight. Her destination today is Teller 47, a hilly research site twenty miles farther from Nome than Teller 27. The goal is to help a colleague, the geomorphologist Joel Rowland. The day before, Rowland had suffered a huge setback: he lost all of his samples for one of his data collection sites.

Rowland and four other team members had spent the two weeks before Wilson arrived collecting soil carbon samples in the field sites around Nome. But on their flight home to Los Alamos, some had gone missing. If the baggage handlers had spilled the dirt collected from Teller 47 onto the runway, it's hard to imagine them being overly concerned by a few tablespoons of dirt on the tarmac, but those accidental molehills were in fact mountains of data. To help Rowland out, Wilson agreed to go out and collect another set of samples, and she seemed invigorated by the mission. "Honestly, I love working with a big team," she says. The truck shudders a bit between the potholes and "Full Throttle." Wilson responds by pressing harder on the gas.

From the driver's-side window of the F-150, a number of gold-mining barges can be seen chugging out of the port of Nome between two long jetties: rush hour on the Bering Sea. The route from Nome to Teller 47 heads north. Not far from the outskirts of town, a band of fog is breaking over a range of 3,000-foot peaks like a wave in the ocean. "Kougarok is just on the other side," says Wilson, pointing east. The roads are empty, although she occasionally passes families who have climbed into the hills to collect blueberries. Wilson keeps her eyes peeled for grizzlies, which she hasn't seen yet on this trip, and stops on a bridge over a river to watch the salmon swimming upstream. A few fish that have spawned and died are bobbing in the eddies. "This project is like living through a *National Geographic* special," Wilson says. "It's the coolest thing I've ever done."

AFTER HER BOSS AT the Fisher Body Company plant told Wilson that she had the chops to become the company's first female plant manager, Wilson quit. By then she'd been working in the factory for two years. "I think I felt like I'd proven to myself that I could survive anything if I had to," she recalls. Even with her father's tuition discount, she couldn't bring herself to return to the University of Michigan. She "needed to get the hell out of there and get away from men for a while." For her senior year of college, she paid out-of-pocket with money she'd saved working in the factory. Returning to the live oaks, eucalyptus, and all-female students of Mills was more than worth it.

It was 1978, and the computer revolution had spilled into the mainstream. Every large company and corporation in America was moving their operations, logistics, and planning branches to computers. American life was being digitized as fast as businesses could snap up the coders to do the work. With this as the backdrop, Wilson took a coding class in college and found a new passion. "I loved math and I love languages. But here I could use math and symbols and words together to tell a machine to create answers. Instead of solving for a single variable, I was solving for systems," Wilson explains. The June that she graduated, Mill's campus swarmed with recruiters from Chevron—then Standard Oil—and a local military defense company. "I think they offered jobs to every girl with coding experience." Wilson got two offers and picked Chevron.

They hired her to write the script, but soon her gift of

logic rose to the surface. Chevron assigned Wilson to a team of three tasked with designing a program that could track where all of their oil went and how it was being traded. From refineries, the oil was sent out via a national network of pipelines and trucks to distributors and sub-distributors before finally arriving at gas stations. Wilson's team was assigned the job of digitizing the entire tracking operation. "It played to my strengths," Wilson says. "I'm good at seeing systems and how they fit together."

She was given a cubicle by the window on the twenty-fourth floor of a skyscraper in Market Center in downtown San Francisco. Wilson is humble about her work, insisting it wasn't complex coding because it didn't require solving multiple differential equations the way climate models do. But for a twenty-four-year-old just out of college, building a computer program that tracked supply for one of the country's biggest oil companies was a thrill. "It was sort of amazing," Wilson says. "Watching it count the barrels once we were through was actually a real rush." They were observing money move in million-dollar increments. But as with her factory job, achieving success made Wilson's feet itch. Around the fall of 1980, she was reading a James A. Michener novel called *Centennial* that told the story of the Great Basin from prehistoric times to the present. The passages are rich in descriptions of geologic and hydrologic processes:

A wall of water would fan out across the plains, engulfing both the river and its tributaries. Churning, roaring, twisting, it would scour everything before it as it scratched and clawed its way eastward. In the space of an afternoon, such a flood might carve away deposits which had required ten million years to accumulate.

Wilson was transfixed—captivated by water and geology's power. At the time, her roommate from college had enrolled in a cultural anthropology PhD program at Berkeley, just across the bay. "I've always been a bit impulsive," Wilson says. "I mean, I didn't know what the hell I was doing." But feeling unsettled at Chevron, she filled out an application to Berkeley's geology program and took the Graduate Record Examinations (GREs), a requirement for entry. With an undergraduate degree in math and a minor in theater arts, she had no science coursework under her belt. "Frankly, there wasn't much reason for the department to take me," she admits. But she'd scored high in analytical skills on her GRE tests and had a demonstrable track record in applied coding, which benefited her application. By the late seventies, the geosciences had recognized that modeling earth system processes empowered them to reassemble the past while also looking into the future.

For her first year at Berkeley, Wilson took classes to get what amounted to her bachelor's degree in geology. One class was chemistry. "I practically screamed when I learned how to make a battery from lemons!" she exclaims. Although some climate scientists get their master's degrees first and then work toward their PhDs, Wilson opted instead to go straight for her PhD. Overall, this education path takes on the order of seven years. By 1983, the end of her second year, she'd advanced far enough in her graduate coursework that she needed to start thinking of her dissertation, a project required of all PhD candidates that proves a scientist's expertise by advancing their field into novel territory. The student's adviser usually helps them select a topic of study.

"Having a good early mentor makes a huge difference in your career path," Wilson maintains. She says that she doesn't know any high-level scientists who didn't benefit from working beneath a widely acclaimed mentor. Wilson would eventually work for William E. Dietrich, whom she describes as the single most productive source of modern geomorphology. Dietrich, in turn, studied with Thomas Dunne, who modernized the concept of hillslope hydrology and who had studied alongside Luna Leopold, the man responsible for setting up the U.S. Geological Survey's river monitoring system, a network of sensors that measure real-time flow information on most of the nation's major waterways. Wilson calls these men the founding fathers of modern hydrology. But none of these were her first mentor.

That was George Brimhall, a brilliant man, though not the one who ultimately most advanced her career. Under his supervision, she labored in a lab trying to understand how silver deposits form. After untold hours of peering through a microscope, she made little headway toward Brimhall's objective and he told her: "It's time to shit or get off the pot," according to Wilson. Frustrated and exhausted, Wilson went so far as applying for a job with the oil company ARCO in Austin, Texas. She thought she'd earn her master's degree in geology, give up on her pursuit of a PhD, and be done with school forever.

Then, a few weeks before she left for Houston, a geomorphology professor five years her senior, Bill Dietrich, asked if she'd be interested in joining him and a few students on a sampling trip to Wyoming. He was studying sediment transport in rivers. Wilson had taken a class with Dietrich and liked him. Somewhere deep inside, she also knew she wasn't entirely ready to abandon school. Maybe, she hoped, Dietrich could give her a path forward.

"Serendipity, luck, and meeting great people—that's what success requires," Wilson says. "It's not like I controlled my own destiny. Nobody does. That trip is the reason I'm here now."

athrop, Bolton, and Jin have spent the past hour digging. They're at Teller 47 and, having hiked into the site where Rowland had collected samples a week earlier, are already hard at work digging up a six-foot-deep pit he and his team had dug and then filled back in. It's a misty day, and across a braided stream, spindrift is blowing into the clouds from the tops of peaks barely visible through the fog.

"We want to know how carbon is transported in the landscape," Wilson says. "How old is it? How vulnerable is it to decomposition? And as it defrosts with climate change, will it drive the generation of CO_2 and methane in the atmosphere?" She's sitting on the bank above the pit, contentedly munching through an olive loaf sandwich while Lathrop and Bolton work in the pit below.

As with every research effort with NGEE Arctic, Rowland's team chose this site intentionally. It sits by a patch of willows at the toe of a solifluction lobe, the name for the peculiar sloughing of soil that happens most places in the Arctic where there are hills. From the top of the hills, the soil rolls downhill over millennia, grabbing any grass it touches at the surface and shoving it deeper into the permafrost. From a distance these lobes look like eyebrows stacked on top of each other—a cascade of dirt avalanches falling in geologic time. Rowland's hypothesis is that in the place where they pile up at the foot of each hill is a dense trove of carbon just waiting to be emitted.

But the process by which how solifluction lobes form isn't well understood and therefore isn't represented in global climate models at all. To figure out if they should be in models, NGEE Arctic was collecting soil at different layers of the solifluction lobe. Back at Los Alamos, the team would then use radiocarbon dating to get the age of the soil and also estimate how much carbon it stored. Just as with the ice wedge polygons they studied in Utqiagvik and the soil moisture they were studying elsewhere on the Seward Peninsula, NGEE Arctic's observations on specific solifluction lobes could be scaled up to the greater Arctic: one more equation in the models.

"If you think about it, the decomposition process in the permafrost has been moving in fits and starts for tens of thousands of years," Bolton says of the roots and plant matter that are decomposing, thereby endowing the soil with the carbon that plants have taken up over a lifetime of photosynthesis. "But now it's about to hit full gas. We're close to a tipping point." Standing beside a cross-section of ancient dirt, he and Wilson describe how permafrost—and solifluction lobes in particular—acts as a carbon sink.

Every summer, grass grows and then starts to decompose. But because the growing seasons are so short in the Arctic, the grass doesn't decompose completely. When winter returns, the microbes in the soil that break down the carbon in the plants become sluggish and the respiration process—you can think of it as bacterial farts—slows to a crawl. Over time, the sloughing of the solifluction lobes rolls the grass and buries the layer of partially decomposed organic matter deeper into the permafrost, where it's colder and the carbon storage is far more stable. Bolton compares this process to a savings account. Unlike in non-Arctic climates, where plants grow, die, and decompose all within a single calendar year, in the Arctic they only grow and die, leaving all that carbon available for decomposition when the climate warms. Now that the climate is warming, the ancient grass is becoming more available to decompose.

"How can you not love dirt!" Lathrop says, before sharing a story of a college classmate who loved dirt so much he had a key for soil identification tattooed to his thigh. She's standing in the pit in rubber boots and poking the soil with a trowel. "Look, there's time right there!"

The soil is so rich in peat that it smells like we're sitting on the rim of a bottle of scotch whiskey. Wilson and the other scientists, who have all done their fair share of digging, now crowd around the pit's edge, trying to decipher a pattern from the layers of dirt. They're looking for a story, some signature that tells them how the lobes move and form. Layers exist but they're not cleanly striated, as you might find in the Grand Canyon. Instead, it's like looking at a cross-section of a smooshed Swiss roll. Lathrop often says that science is messy, and that idea is reinforced here. The layers are muddled, bent, folded over each other, and sometimes just disappear. Bolton estimates that all these changes to the soil's structure took place over 10,000 years—20,000 at the base. Maybe 50,000. Which means that Lathrop is standing on grass that grew when woolly mammoths roamed the Arctic, and it is only just now starting to decompose.

"That hill slopes and solifluction lobes could be an important contribution to storing and burying this carbon is a new idea," Wilson says, then unwittingly echoes a modern take on the old debate that drew Keeling into climate science decades earlier. "So the question is how fast is the carbon sequestration in relation to the decomposition and release? If plants become more productive because it's warmer in the Arctic, then can they start to take up more carbon and maybe they'll balance the decomposition rate? We don't know that. That's what other people in NGEE Arctic are trying to understand."

Bolton now jumps into the hole beside Lathrop. "I think I

just threw out my back and then threw it back into place," he jokes. Science aside for the moment, they start kidding about holding a NGEE Arctic Olympics, where teams could compete in digging pits, hurdling tussocks, probing snow, and collecting soil moisture measurements the fastest. The question of how to sample the soil so it's most useful for Rowland comes up. Remember, this isn't Wilson's area of expertise, and in watching the gentle way she navigates her relationship with Lathrop is instructive on how she views her role as a mentor: an enabler who helps guide her pupils' paths by giving them access to experiences.

This is Lathrop's third trip to Alaska. On this one, she'll stay for three weeks, work upward of sixteen hours a day, and have a single day off. "This is our one shot for the summer to get the data," Lathrop says. "We've got to hustle." If Wilson's job is to find stories within the mountains of data she and her team collects, Lathrop's job is to do the reporting. One of her main jobs before coming north was organizing all the equipment needed to travel. Before leaving on this trip, she spent two months preparing. Her office in Los Alamos was so full of gear she could barely walk into it. There were soil moisture probes, extra rubber boots, shovels, piles of snacks, Nalgene bottles for collecting samples, a drone, spare Pelican cases—all of it eventually FedExed to Alaska or taken there in carry-on luggage by the team.

Wilson relies on Lathrop for much more than trip prep. In the field, Lathrop shoulders most of the physical burden of collecting data. In the lab, she's responsible for processing it. That includes drying out soil samples and then creating spreadsheets to organize the data for later algorithmic analysis. Wilson has also encouraged Lathrop to be the coauthor and even the first author on scientific papers, an honor usually reserved for PhD candidates or driven researchers with master's degrees. Lathrop holds a bachelor's degree in environmental science with a minor in math but doesn't consider herself a climate scientist. ("My work contributes to climate science," she says.) Wilson disagrees. She says, "I simply could not do what I do without Emma. She's invaluable."

As far as entry-level climate science positions go, Lathrop's is an especially good one, and therefore competitive. Wilson says that she gets about a dozen calls or emails a year from students who heard about NGEE Arctic and want to join the project. For a twenty-two-year-old, the pay, about $50,000 a year, is excellent, and the experience even better. Traveling to exotic locations for work makes her friends and family jealous, but what makes her experience with NGEE Arctic so valuable professionally is that it allows her to practice science outside the narrow confines of academia. For all its emphasis on precision and methodology, science is fundamentally messy. Nothing demonstrates that as clearly as fieldwork.

Six small flags come out, and Wilson and Lathrop start discussing where in the Swiss roll it is most useful to sample soil and whether they should clean the shovel between samples. Lathrop, who was here when Rowland's team took samples the first time, says they didn't wash the shovel because the threat of cross-contaminating the soils didn't matter. The lab work was not sensitive enough to be able to differentiate, she says. For a while Wilson considers Lathrop's perspective, asking questions and mulling the answers. Ultimately, though, Wilson's fastidiousness wins the day and she overrules her mentee. They'll sample the slow way, the more time-consuming, more precise way—with clean shovels.

BILL DIETRICH, WILSON'S MENTOR, studied sediment transport on Muddy Creek, a clear river that flows through Wyoming's high desert just north of the Utah border. For two weeks Wilson camped with Dietrich and his team in the desert, drinking cheap beer around a campfire at night and discussing the results of the day under stars so numerous, they washed the sky in blue light. They bathed in the freezing creek and invented new tools for sampling and techniques, like the string of small nets they cast downstream in the flow to measure how much and where the river was moving sediment. For Wilson, this was science as she imagined it when first reading Michener almost four years earlier. The grit required to enjoy the outdoors, the temperament necessary to collect precise data in an uncontrolled environment—it suited her. "Cathy had the rare ability to observe patterns in the real world," remembered Dietrich. "She had the spark of somebody who loved the field. You can't teach that."

When Wilson and the team returned to Berkeley, Dietrich asked her if she'd be interested in becoming his second PhD student. The previous year, the winter of 1982, had been exceptionally wet and triggered a series of landslides that killed dozens up and down California's coast. Dietrich was interested in creating a model that could predict when the risk of landslides was highest, essentially an avalanche advisory forecast for moving mud. At that time, most scientists fell into either the camp of observationalist or modeler. Dietrich wanted Wilson to participate in both. "Observational science should be used to build and improve models, and models should help tell us where we should be collecting observations," Dietrich said years later. "It's a feedback loop." Given Wilson's clear love for fieldwork, her math skills, and her ability to code, she was a perfect fit for a project that would prove to be far ahead of its time.

"I remember when I showed her the research site," Dietrich says. "She walked out there and could see all these rolling hills and the Pacific and said, 'You get to work here?'"

The observation site was in Mount Tamalpais, a protected area on the north end of San Francisco Bay. After a year peering through an electron microscope in a lab to try and decipher the building blocks of silver deposits, a project she found tedious, the decision to join Dietrich was an easy one. "Curiosity drove me. I wanted to know how things work and wanted to figure out how you measure things to figure out how things work," she says.

The factors that trigger landslides became Wilson's dissertation. To help Dietrich, she took a job as a teacher's assistant for Dietrich's undergraduate geomorphology class. She spent the next five years studying landslides, which, after an undergraduate degree, is the average time it takes a scientist to earn a PhD. Her first two years were dedicated to collecting observational data. She bored dozens of holes into hillsides, places where she could measure the water pressure at different points in the drainage. To offset the labor one day, she invited the class of undergraduates she was serving as a teaching assistant for to come out to help.

During the field trip, they were installing PVC pipes into the hillside, making tiny wells that Wilson used to measure water pressure in the soil and bedrock, when a six-foot-four student named Kent Rich took the bentonite that he was using to create a seal on an instrument and as a joke wiped it down the front of Wilson's jeans. "What the hell do you think you're doing?" Wilson asked, aghast, while Kent laughed in glee. "It was the first time I'd really seen him."

About a year later, when Wilson was thirty-one, they were married. Kent, who wasn't interested in acquiring a PhD, agreed to support Wilson in her career. According to Wilson, "Our agreement when we got married was he wanted kids but I wasn't so sure. 'Okay,' I said, 'I'll have kids, but you have to be willing to be the primary caregiver.'" From the outset, Wilson made clear the importance of her career. Any time the rain came, she rushed out to Mount Tamalpais State Park to take measurements.

The first winter of her field research was dry, and other than providing the necessary period of time for correcting her instrument's flaws, the data did little to solve the riddle of why landslides happened. But the second year was one of the wettest on record. It rained almost nonstop for three months, triggering landslides up and down California's coast. "You never know what you're going to get," says Dietrich. "She got lucky."

"We'd slept in the car after a round of measurements, and I pretty much had pneumonia by the end," Wilson says. "It was miserable and wonderful." Wilson's site never had a landslide, but she measured in the real world what her models would later determine is the oversaturation point at which a landslide occurs on a slope. Using her observations, she built a simplified numerical model of the hill-slopes that was cutting edge for the time. The coding took her nearly a year to complete. "The models were murderously slow back then, but they'd let her connect A to D," says Dietrich. "Her data set was quite unusual. Unknowingly, she was studying what we now call the critical zone, the skin on the earth."

By the end of her time in Berkeley, Wilson had produced just one paper ("The greatest shame of my life is that I only produced one paper from my PhD," she recalls with a laugh, because its common for PhD candidates to publish two or even three research papers from their dissertations). The article combined both modeling and field observations, a novelty at the time but is becoming more common in the field, as demonstrated by NGEE Arctic. She'd also proven herself a leader within Dietrich's program. Dietrich said she was essentially running his entire research division. "What Bill taught me about combining modeling and observations pretty much got me every job I've had ever since," Wilson says.

Around the time she received her PhD in 1988, Australia's top research institute, the Commonwealth Scientific and Industrial Research Organisation, or CSIRO, wanted to develop a model that could capture how complex terrain influenced water flow. Nobody had done it well before, and for a country with so much desert, understanding water's flow cycle was critical. CSIRO hired Wilson when she was seven months pregnant, and she and Kent moved across the Pacific. Within two months of starting the job, she'd given birth, and was back to work three days later. "We couldn't afford not to," she says. "Kent didn't have a job and I was the breadwinner." They slept on a bare mattress in an empty apartment. Kent watched their daughter, Talerra, and Wilson worked. She tells a heartbreaking story of returning from a work trip to New Zealand that lasted almost two weeks. When she went to hug Talerra, her daughter cried. "All the travel hasn't only been a good thing," Wilson acknowledges. "It has required sacrifices."

At CSIRO, Wilson studied how agriculture and forestry impacted water quality and how clearing eucalyptus forests was increasing the salinity of the landscape—studies that would be used to influence policy in the future. But her primary focus was how logging and wildfires impacted erosion in Tasmanian forests. ("The conclusions were pretty much what you'd expect: logging increased erosion," she says.) But the work caught her superiors' eyes nonetheless. In 1995, CSIRO made her the first female program manager of the Cooperative Research Centre for Catchment Hydrology, a multiagency institute where she ran one of four large programs worth millions of dollars. By then, Wilson and Kent had been in Australia for eleven years. They had two kids now, Talerra and Dylan, and home was calling.

In December 1999, Wilson accepted a job as a research scientist at Los Alamos National Laboratory, and from New Mexico's high desert would put herself on a course toward Alaska's frozen ground.

9

Wilson makes no attempt to hide her affection for the people she works with. "They determine whether or not you love or hate this job," Wilson says. It's a sentiment echoed by all of her colleagues. In the lab, climate science is a constant collaboration; in the field, trusting each other can quite literally be a matter of life or death.

It's now one of the final mornings of Wilson's two-week research trip. She, Lathrop, Bolton, and Jin are hiking up a long ridge. Their goal is to collect soil moisture measurements and soil samples from Teller 27. The soil samples will deliver yet another piece of the Arctic puzzle. Their interest here is whether the dirt is loamy or peaty or sandy. Does it drain? Is it wet? Is it dry? Can these metrics be observed from the NASA planes? Can they be seen from space? Teller 27 "feels like a *Star Wars* set," Emma Lathrop says—empty, remote, wild, grand. To avoid tripping, she walks like a cat in a puddle, placing each of her heavy boots on top of tussock clumps.

This is Bolton's favorite site in the winter. It's easy to see why. The view here is 360°, with the Sinuk River draining along the foot of the low hills to the south before draining into the Bering Sea, visible in the distance. The day is bright and breezy, the saw grass bending in waves with every gust, each blade reflecting light like a fish's scale. When the scientists near the ridgetop, a herd of twenty or thirty musk oxen snort an alarm as they all turn, squaring their shoulders up as they watch the approaching scientists. Musk oxen aren't aggressive animals, but a phalanx of several hundred tons of black-furred Arctic bovid is nonetheless intimidating. "Musk oxen survive on moss," Bolton says, hushed and mystified. "In the winter, they stand in the exact same place, just getting blown about by forty- or fifty-mile-an-hour winds." The musk oxen are standing directly in the path to the research site, so Wilson pulls up a map of the site on her iPad and makes the quick decision to go off course, bushwhacking a wide detour around the animals on a route that is no harder to walk through than the original one—a nice perk of the tundra. Somebody comments that there's something special about starting the day with a commute shared with a herd of musk oxen.

Of her colleagues here, Xiaoying Jin has worked with Wilson the least. The pair met only days earlier. Jin is a Chinese doctoral student who came to the United States to study with Bolton's colleague, the esteemed Arctic scientist Vladimir E.

Romanovsky. Jin is a small woman with dark hair that she has tucked beneath a wool sun hat. She grew up in the desert in northeast China, and decided as a young girl to study desertification after she watched the creek in her backyard dry up. "There were fish there when I was very little," she recalled one day while sampling. "And then suddenly the fish were gone. And then the water disappeared too." After studying the underlying causes of desertification as an undergraduate, she earned a master's degree from the Chinese Academy of Sciences but struggled to find an adviser in China who would support her doctoral work on permafrost thaw. "They all preferred a strong man who could hike and carry lots of things," she said. She applied to universities in the United States, and through the NGEE Arctic project and Romanovsky, at the University of Alaska Fairbanks, she came to the field with Bolton. Jin is now in the fifth year of her doctoral studies and focuses on permafrost thaw in Tibet. She hopes to wrap up her studies in the next two or three years.

"I wanted [Jin] to come see the field and meet Cathy," Bolton says. He's now hiking toward the research site, the musk oxen still apparently concerned and staring in his back from afar. "Their research is similar. I also just want her to talk with Cathy because she's a leader in the field. She's gone through some tough stuff to get where she is."

He and Wilson have been working together for nearly a

decade now. The closeness of their relationship is clear. In terms of personalities, they sometimes seem like polar opposites. Bolton is laid-back and quiet, although he hasn't always been that way. "I lost a marriage over being too intense, for being too involved in my work," he says. At the time, he was getting his PhD at the University of Alaska Fairbanks, and he loved it—maybe too much. Every day, Bolton would try to teach his computer to do something new, design a bit of code or figure out an equation that he hadn't been able to solve before. But he couldn't see past the work; it consumed him and his life. The divorce broke his heart. "Since then I've tried to do a better job following the advice my adviser gave me, 'Recognize which of the balls that you're juggling will break if you drop them and which will bounce,'" Bolton, who is now happily remarried, says. "Because you can't juggle them all."

Bolton says that he sometimes worries about Wilson because it's clear how many balls she's juggling and he's never seen her treat any like they could bounce. "She's got an incredibly tough job. I think a lot of that is because she has such high expectations for herself," he says. After so many years of working together with Wilson, he can recognize when she gets tired because her perfectionism softens. She starts to say "Whatever" a lot, he notices. When that happens, Bolton takes on some of her responsibilities as a leader by stepping up and making decisions for the team.

Fieldwork comes naturally for Bolton. He grew up in Wyoming, lives in Fairbanks, Alaska, and has spent a good percentage of his career working alone in the field. He estimates around two months a year are spent in the wild, which has afforded him plenty of time for close calls. His first and worst came in the Seward Peninsula almost three decades earlier. Bolton was working on his dissertation with a Chinese student, a master of science, and they were staying together in a cabin for three weeks. To reach the field site, the two had to cross the river each morning in a canoe. It was during the spring melt and the river was full of icebergs drifting downstream. One morning Bolton was suffering from sun poisoning from too many hours of direct sunlight the day before, and a strong wind was blowing downstream. It blew Bolton and his colleague's canoe, with the men still in it, on top of an iceberg. They were carried a hundred meters downstream before they succeeded in pulling the boat off the ice. Had it capsized, they might have drowned. Had they gotten wet, they would have been at risk of hypothermia. "We should have died three times on that trip," Bolton says. The other two were when they spilled white gas all over the counter of a log cabin and it caught fire, and the third was when they almost had a chimney fire in the small cabin. Ever since, Bolton has become the team's safety leader, teaching a course on it to each member of NGEE Arctic who joins him in the field. Mentorship, he says, is a big part of his job. It's also one of his favorites.

"I'm in academia, and that's a big difference between my work and Cathy's. I'm expected to advise," Bolton says. When taking on students, whether working toward their master's or doctorate, the first question Bolton asks is: "Why do you want to get a graduate degree?" He wants to work with people who are self-starters, who know exactly what science question they're trying to answer. He agrees that having initiative is important and adds that programming skills are a plus. But one of the most important aspects for Wilson is fit. What's a candidate's personality type? Can they adapt on the fly? One example of a good answer to this question came from a recent hire. Wilson asked her how comfortable she was fixing instruments in the field.

"She said, 'Oh, I grew up on a farm, and we were always tinkering with all types of things, and I've been flying these atmospheric instruments on planes. I don't mind trying to fix the instruments at all,'" Wilson says. She loved the answer, and she loved her confidence. "This kind of work takes a high degree of self-confidence, because I'm relying on people to take care of themselves."

Both she and Bolton recognize that, as exciting as the job can be, climate science involves a fair amount of drudgery. "No matter what level you're at, even senior scientist, the job requires a lot of tedious work," she explains. "Sometimes people get into this field and realize: 'I don't want to be looking at data sheets all day,'" Wilson says. "Once they learn it's not all camping, not all just being out in the field, and that 90 percent of the time you're sitting in front of the computer, they want out."

For example, Bolton and Wilson ask their master's and bachelor's students to help with quality assurance, which means clicking through spreadsheets to make certain that every decimal on hundreds of different measurements is in the right place. Data is the main ingredient from which all science is based, and must be collected accurately. For this reason, they both try to get their young scientists time in the field. "People who collect their own data have much more interest in doing a good job processing it," Wilson says, echoing the passion she first felt while studying erosion with Dietrich in Wyoming.

One real struggle is staying focused and detail oriented during the long hours of data collection. The thrilling moments of fieldwork tend to be far and few between. Lathrop says if she had to draw a graph plotting excitement during the winter sampling campaign, it would look like your bottom row of teeth: a sharp point on one end when the helicopter comes, followed by a long, flat line where they do the work of probing the snow, then another incisor when the helicopter returns. These are highly intelligent people conducting important research, but they're not above devising ways to pass the time. Fancy gummy bears help Stan Wullschleger focus. Lathrop listens to podcasts. Bolton takes an inordinate amount of pride in keeping the lines between his flags perfectly straight, in writing his measurements neatly in the journal (with a line through his sevens, European-style), and likes to invent little games.

"What do you think this one will be?" Bolton says, now probing the soil along a transect. Wilson, Lathrop and Jin, all working within earshot, wager guesses. The consensus is 35. Bolton guesses 27, nails it, and gives a gleeful snort.

Several hours later, Wilson and Lathrop use bread knives to cut through moss and saw into the peat. These soil samples will show the density and texture of the dirt, a key metric in understanding how fast the soil drains and ultimately whether the thawing permafrost emits carbon or methane. They carefully set each sample into a tin for transport. If the dirt loses its structure, it becomes a different sample entirely and not very useful for determining how water flows through the soil type in situ. "You only get one shot," Lathrop says as she places a sample that looks like a brownie into a tin.

"Oooh, you go, girl!" Wilson tells her.

By design, to encourage young students to move on, Lathrop's position should last only two years. But she's going on three now. The trouble is she doesn't know what she wants to do next. It's likely to be science, but maybe not Arctic science. "You realize the gaps pretty quickly between the theoretical and applied," Lathrop says. She adds that NGEE Arctic has taught her that scientists go into the field with a fixed set of ideas, but the realities on the ground often force them to improvise. "It taught me to do my best. Honestly, everyone is out there trying to do their best. What matters more than anything is that you collect your data consistently," she says.

Lathrop tells a story about the last time Wilson collected data from Teller 27. They wanted to get information on moisture and other soil properties, so they collected the soil in baggies, changing its porosity. Wilson understood the samples might not be useful for soil density studies, but they could be useful in other ways. It turned out to be useful for both. "I thought it would have been ruined for our purposes, but it wasn't," Lathrop reflects. "Sometimes you have to invent a path and then stick to it, because there's always value in comparisons." The most important thing, she stresses, is measuring something that speaks to the current condition of the place. With that, they can measure again to see if it's changing, figure out why, and come up with a way to show where the environment is going.

This exchange strikes Wilson as exactly right, and she uses it to segue into a story about taking a geology class in college. The professor brought her into a room with rocks on every shelf. From one, he pulled a black rock about the size of her fist and told her that he'd found it on the side of the road. "'What is it?' he asked me," Wilson tells Lathrop. "I came up with this crazy complicated explanation about how the rock formed and why it was there, and the professor just laughed. 'It's road tar,' he said. Sometimes you need to look for the most obvious explanation," she says.

The truth in this wisdom becomes particularly evident later in the afternoon. The team moves to a site a long hike from the ridgetop. It sits on the edge of a wide river valley, a half mile from a ribbon of cold water that's burbled down from the high peaks to the east. The site is pocked with holes four feet deep. How did they get there? Why were they there? Was it possible that the Sinuk River flowed up here and some abnormal flow patterns bored the holes in the dirt? Could it be glacial till, rocks moved by the ice and deposited after it melted? Maybe. But probably, Wilson says, it was mining equipment that dug these holes.

"I think it was a tractor from an old gold mining operation digging here," Wilson says. Although much of Alaska is wild and untrammeled, Wilson notes that "man has impacted almost every inch of the Seward." Though not visible to the naked eye, the same is true about the very air around her.

With that, Wilson gets up and slings over her shoulder a pack heavy with samples, each a precious key to predicting how man is reshaping the atmosphere and global climate. As she hikes back to her truck across permafrost that has only begun to thaw in her lifetime, Wilson quietly starts to hum the DeJ Loaf song "Back Up." "Oh-oh, ya, ya. Back up off me. Back up off me," she raps, working steps atop tussocks into a dance.

10

I t's far from Arctic cold, but it's a brisk Tuesday night when Wilson walks into a glass-walled office space in a strip mall in Los Alamos and busies herself shuffling chairs around until each is just so. Displayed on a supersize monitor behind her is the opening slide of a presentation she's about to give to forty high schoolers: "THE MELTING ARCTIC: HOW WILL IT AFFECT US?"

It's been five months since Wilson commuted through a herd of musk oxen to a research site; two months since collecting a vial of air from an isolated research station in Utqiagvik, Alaska; one month since attending an international meeting of the world's top Arctic climate modelers in Iceland; and two weeks since she traveled to San Francisco to meet with the entire NGEE Arctic team. By then she'd lost $1,000 worth of eyeglasses during her travels. "A bit scatterbrained from the trips," she says in her defense. Just days earlier she and the modelers had met again and distilled the data she'd collected in Utqiagvik on ice wedge polygon thaw into an equation that she and the team felt confident would end up in global climate models—a small win for the project. At the same time she'd heard back from higher-ups at Los Alamos National Laboratory. In a disappointing decision, they'd declined her proposal to turn the lab into the country's preeminent research facility focused on climate solutions, opting instead to renew their commitment to weapons creation and more traditional defense-related technologies. (Although LANL studies weapons, infectious diseases, nonproliferation, and many other national security threats, and despite many of the Department of Energy's own scientists insisting climate change is a national security threat, they haven't yet made commensurate investments in climate research. The reasons are political.).

"She's a boomer!" A spindly teenager laughs as he walks into the room. He's reading the first lines of the short bio that Wilson wrote to recount how a math nerd who studied theater arts in college, built General Motors trucks on a factory line during college, and worked for Chevron became a climate scientist at one of the world's most distinguished research institutions. The kids, who either don't know or don't care that Wilson's in earshot, start blaming her generation for climate change—"boomer shaming," they actually call it. Now it's Wilson's turn to laugh. "It doesn't hurt my feelings, because I was much more of an activist at their age than they are," she says.

By her own admission, after having already worked a twelve-hour day, she's exhausted. "At some point in your career, you spend less of your day-to-day doing the touchstone of science and more of your job is spent in other roles," she says. "Now so much of what I do is acting as an ambassador of science." Explaining her research to others is an essential part of her job, and not one that comes naturally to most scientists. But giving a presentation to a group of kids who will inherit the future climate—and may yet have a chance to change it—is critically important to her. Specifically, she wants them to know why shrubs growing in a previously unvegetated watershed two hours northwest of Nome, Alaska, may soon be a reason that snow stops falling at the ski resort behind Los Alamos. Or why, each summer, wildfires keep burning more American lands than at any point in recent history—like the burn that caused these kids to evacuate their homes ten years earlier. Or why Australia was at that moment ablaze with startling intensity. The forty kids came mostly for the extra credit.

Wilson's first slides are orienting; they're environmental, sociological, or geopolitical. "The Arctic is warming twice as fast as the rest of the world," she tells the kids. "Now I'm going to take you on a little time trip." She hits "play" on an animation that shows a map of the world with mean annual temperature imposed on top of it. If it's warmer than the mean annual temperature, the colors tint red. If it's cooler, they tint blue. The animation starts at 1850, a significant year, because it marks when the fossil fuel–burning engines that powered the industrial revolution began their global spread. That year was relatively cool. So were most of the next hundred. But then, around the middle of the twentieth century, the colors began to warm—from light blues to neutral whites—until soon, in the sixties, orange flashes. By the 1990s, red blobs spot the globe. But where it gets really interesting is in the final few seconds before the animation reaches the present day.

The Arctic, which transitioned to a deepening red over the past two decades, suddenly shades purple, like the world has been punched on its head and swelling is emanating from the bruise. "It's 6 degrees Celsius [10.8 degrees Fahrenheit] warmer in the Arctic than it was three decades ago," Wilson says. She shows pictures of polar bears clinging to melting icebergs, and roads and buildings completely destroyed by the upheaval of thawed permafrost. She doesn't show hurricanes or intensifying cyclones, flooding, the desertification of China, or rising seas in Miami. She doesn't have to. By now the teenagers have fallen quiet. They get the point.

"We still don't know how much greenhouse gas will be produced by this process of permafrost thawing. How fast it will be emitted. And whether it will be CO_2, which is a weak greenhouse gas, or methane, which is four times stronger," Wilson says, now pointing to a chart that shows the volume of carbon and methane stored in permafrost. But, she states emphatically, annual emissions from the permafrost alone could be on the scale of the world's fourth-largest economy.

Wilson tells them a little about how she wound up as a researcher at Los Alamos. She skips the harshest stories from her time at the factory, but she shares that when she first started in this career, she was one of only a few women in science. Now, she says, the gender ratio is nearly balanced. "That makes me incredibly proud," she says. "There is more to do, but we're moving in the right direction."

With that, the kids start to pepper her with questions. And a gray-haired scientist from the generation that oversaw the greatest increase in atmospheric CO_2 in geologic time explains to a generation of kids who will bear the brunt of that change what their future will likely hold. Each question Wilson answers earnestly and with great thought. She wants to make something very clear: people changed the course of global climate once already. We can do it again.

ACKNOWLEDGMENTS

During the fact-checking process of the book, Cathy asked me how I write stories about subjects that I have no previous knowledge of. It's a fair question but it's a bit off the mark. My wife, Turin, studies plant physiology at LANL and works in the same building as Cathy, even applying her specialties to NGEE Arctic's sister project, NGEE Tropics. Because of Turin, I didn't come to climate science completely naïve. But what I want to emphasize here is my answer to Cathy's question: I'm a reporter. What's written in this book isn't my knowledge. It's my sources'.

To that end, I owe Cathy an enormous debt of gratitude. In addition to inviting me to Alaska and giving me the unbelievable opportunity to spend a week in a landscape that may be completely different by the time my kids get to see it, she spent hours with me on the phone and in coffee shops explaining her life, her career, and the choices that forged the path she's walked. I hope this book accurately tells the story of how this remarkable woman ended up where she is. I also hope that story inspires others to follow a similar path.

Cathy, of course, wasn't my only source for this book. I want to thank Bob Bolton, Xiaoying Jin, and especially Emma Lathrop for tolerating my ignorance and answering my many questions. I want to thank Jeremy Fyke, Dylan Harp, and Adam Atchley for talking me through climate modeling; Richard Somerville and Michael Prather for their perspective on the history and evolution of climate science; Stan Wullschleger for his take on the evolution and success of NGEE Arctic; Larry Hinzman for his take on Arctic research; and Charles Poling for initially connecting me with Wilson.

Personally, I want to thank my wife, Turin, who is always so patient with me and the distracted mindset that writing puts me into. My parents, Bonnie and Paul, and her parents, Ben and Libby, gave me the time to write by watching our kids, Bridger and Tallie.

And I want to thank my editor, Emily Simonson. Not only did she approach me to see if I'd be interested in undertaking what has been a truly fascinating project, but she's been a steady hand in this very unstable time. Both her big-picture edits and her line edits have been excellent, and she's been a joy to work with. So, thank you, Emily.

FURTHER READING

The path to a career in climate science can be incredibly varied. But if you have an aptitude and interest in math and science, are eager to travel and to contribute to our understanding of the crises created by climate change, and want to work in a rapidly expanding field, consider yourself encouraged. Before you dive in, though, ask yourself a few questions. Does fieldwork interest you? If so, be ready to move for your job, which could take you absolutely anywhere in the world. If you're unattached and adventurous, that could mean months a year in the wilds researching. But if a swashbuckling career doesn't suit your lifestyle, there are plenty of alternative climate-related fields to work in, such as: modeling; lab-based studies on plants, the atmosphere, aerosols, or man-made pollutants; or even conservation work for nonprofits or environmental law. There are also a growing number of universities and colleges that offer programs in hard climate sciences and related fields. A few of the many examples of good places to start looking include Oregon State University; the University of California, Berkeley;

the University of Colorado, Boulder; and Yale. If earning a PhD appeals to you, expect to spend a decade in school. But work options do exist in climate science for those with an undergraduate or master's degree, which generally take four and four more years, respectively, to earn. To see what career opportunities are out there, check out websites like climate careers.com. Salaries can range between entry-level positions paying $30,000 to senior positions like Wilson's that net on the order of $150,000.

Before choosing a school to attend, the best first step is deciding what interests you most. Never before have so many books—novels, investigative nonfiction, textbooks—wrestled so thoughtfully with the question of what the changing climate will do to humanity. Reading these additional resources might help guide your interest in a sprawling field:

- Elizabeth Kolbert, *The Sixth Extinction: An Unnatural History* (New York: Henry Holt, 2014)

  Elizabeth Kolbert's remarkable investigative reporting delivers a deep dive on the five major extinction events earth has experienced. Then it goes deeper on the human-prompted extinction we're witnessing now. Key quote: "By disrupting these systems . . . we're putting our own survival on the line." Maybe the most joyful part of this book is the conclusion, where Kolbert describes witnessing the dismantling of earth's primary eco-systems with the dissociative awareness of a surgeon amputating her own arm. This, she writes, is a unique moment in earth history. Enjoy it.

- Bill McKibbon, *The End of Nature* (New York: Random House, 1989)

  Bill McKibbon wrote this book in the late 1980s, and aside from employing the now seldom-used term "greenhouse effect," it is still every bit as salient as it was then. A swan song to true wild places, this book will give us pride in our world and, if you're lacking, provide you with a reason to try and steer its fate in a new direction.

- Intergovernmental Panel on Climate Change (IPCC) reports (every six to seven years)

  Look, these aren't lighthearted readings. But if you want a summation of all the latest climate science, these internationally produced reports give readers a sense of where the climate is now, how it got here, where it's going, and what, if anything, humans can do to alter its course. Visit https://www.ipcc.ch/reports/.

- Tim Flannery. *The Eternal Frontier: An Ecological History of North America and Its Peoples* (Melbourne, Australia: Textbook Publishing, 2001)

  Really, you could read just about any of Tim Flannery's more than twenty excellent books and learn a great deal about the natural world. This one, an insightful exploration of how North America was repopulated following the asteroid that prompted the global extinction of dinosaurs, just happens to be relevant to North America. Its relevance to climate is that the book details how geology and weather collided to shape North America's climate and how climate has been the primary driver of the continent's biology—both its evolution and extinction.

- Richard Powers, *The Overstory* (New York: W. W. Norton, 2018)

  This astonishing novel looks at the world through the perspective of trees—kind of. Using the stories of memorable characters who all have intimate relationships with trees, Powers's Pulitzer Prize–winning novel gives readers a sense of how our natural world formed and what it may look like after humans leave it. It is simultaneously a depressing and inspiring read.

- Andrew Dessler, *Introduction to Modern Climate Science* (New York: Cambridge University Press, 2012)

  Yes, it's a little drier than the other recommendations on this list. But as promised by the title, this textbook is a quintessential introduction to modern climate science: from the observations that go into the field, to the code that turns those observations into digital representations of the earth itself. If you're ready to dive into the nuts and bolts of the science, start here.

- Nathaniel Rich, *Losing Earth: A Recent History* by (New York: MCD/Farrar, Straus and Giroux, 2019)

  A bleak history of how long we've known about the changing climate and why the political, social, and economic will hasn't been fostered to make any significant changes. In a slice of what this book offers, "Nearly every conversation we have in 2019 about climate change was being held in 1979."

- McKenzie Funk, *Windfall: The Booming Business of Global Warming* (New York: Penguin Press, 2014)

  Disasters create opportunity. But for whom? And who is taking advantage of them? Essentially an economic investigation into the companies who are profiting off climate change, Funk's deeply reported book, frankly, puts one in a sad state of mind. What pulls it back from the brink are profiles of the companies working to creative solutions to mitigate the worst of the damage.

- Naomi Klein, *This Changes Everything: Capitalism vs. The Climate* (New York: Simon & Schuster, 2014)

  A deep dive into how the rise of neoliberalism and the age of climate change are inseparably linked. This big-picture look at the underlying causes of climate change contextualizes the current state of affairs. Consider it essential reading for the field of climate science.

- Carbon Brief: Clear on Climate, CarbonBrief.com

  The editors and writers of this website took upon themselves the tremendous task of untangling how climate models were built.

ABOUT THE AUTHOR

Kyle Dickman is an award-winning journalist, contributing editor at *Outside* magazine, and author of *On the Burning Edge*. He lives with his wife, Turin, and their two kids, Bridger and Tallie, in Los Alamos, New Mexico.